Father Pat Col

Pat Collins, a Dubliner, was ordained a Vincentian in 1971. Afterwards he taught for ten years in a secondary school in Armagh. During that time he became involved with the charismatic and ecumenical movements in Northern Ireland. In 1987 he wrote a book on charismatic spirituality which was published in Italy. More recently he wrote a handbook for prayer groups entitled *Maturing in the Spirit*.

During the early eighties he trained in the U.S.A. as a spiritual director. While there, he felt that he was being called by God both to identify and to repair dangerous breaches in the walls of people's spiritual lives. Since then he has spent most of his time conducting parish renewal programmes as a member of the Vincentian Mission Team. That experience led him to write *Finding Faith in Troubled Times*. He has also participated in many ongoing formation courses for priests. In 1991 he contributed a chapter to *Priestly Development in a Changing World*.

Over the years he has become well known as a broadcaster, international conference speaker and as a writer on psycho-spiritual topics. Besides *Intimacy and the Hungers of the Heart* and *Growing in Health and Grace* – which has since been translated into Italian – Fr. Pat has written *The Joy of Belonging*. Like his many tapes, this latest book aims to help people who want to grow in loving relationship with themselves, others and the Lord. Currently, Fr. Pat is lecturer in spirituality and philosophy at All Hallows College, an international institute for mission and ministry in Dublin.

The Joy
of
Belonging

PAT COLLINS C.M.

CAMPUS PUBLISHING

ISBN 1 873223 90 0

First published 1993

Typeset by Irish Typesetters, Galway.
Printed in the Republic of Ireland by Colour Books Ltd.
Cover photograph courtesy of Bord Fáilte.

Published by

Campus Publishing
26 Tirellan Heights
Galway
Ireland

Contents

Author's Note

In 1986 I wrote *A Daily Prayer to the Holy Spirit*. Shortly afterwards, sixteen other leaflets followed. Some of them were summaries of longer pieces of mine which have been published elsewhere e.g. *Growing in Health and Grace*. Taken together, they covered a wide range of subjects. Each one aimed to take a brief but informative look at an aspect of the Christian life in a way that would be clear, concise and relevant. From the beginning sales of the leaflets far exceeded my expectations.

Some time ago it occurred to me that it might be a good idea to publish the lot in booklet form. Thus, in 1990 All Hallows College issued *Me, You and God*. For convenience sake, it was divided into three main sections. The first, entitled "Me," dealt with the inner life; the second, entitled "You," looked at relationships with other people; the third, entitled "God," focused on awareness of the Divine Presence. Judging by the thousands of copies that have been sold over the past two years, it seemed to meet a need.

More recently, I revised and added to the material in the first edition. However, the format remains much the same. Five new chapters have been added. They are entitled "Emotional self-awareness", "Healthy and unhealthy forms of guilt", "Christian compassion", "Be filled with the Spirit", and "The promises of God".

It is my hope that *The Joy of Belonging* will help you to be inwardly transformed through a growing relationship with yourself, other people and the Lord (cf Rm 12:2). I have found that it is this overlapping sense of connection which is the source of that spiritual joy which G. K. Chesterton described as "the gigantic secret of the Christian".

PART ONE

Me

1. Self-esteem and the love of God

2. Emotional self-awareness

3. A Christian understanding of dreams

4. Suffering T.H.E. Christian way

5. Overcoming stress

6. Crises in life: opportunities for growth

7. Healthy and unhealthy forms of guilt

1. SELF-ESTEEM AND THE LOVE OF GOD

The Importance of Self-esteem

Both the Bible and modern psychology agree that self-esteem is very important.

In Sirach 10:27 we read: "My son, with humility have *self-esteem.*"

This point finds an echo in the teaching of Jesus. In Luke 10:27 he says: "Love your neighbour as yourself."

Modern psychology teaches the same point: that lack of self-acceptance leads to low self-esteem and neurosis. As Jung has written, "What drives people to war with themselves is the suspicion or the knowledge that they consist of two persons in opposition to one another. The conflict may be between the sensual and the spiritual person, or between the ego and the shadow. It is what Faust means when he says: 'Two souls, alas, are housed within my breast.' A neurosis is a splitting of personality."

Like other psychologists, Jung goes on to say that human maturity consists of three inseparable ingredients.

1. Accept yourself

In other words, don't reject any aspect of your personality, not even that part of you that is weak and seems to be unable to live up to your conscious ideals. Have a feeling of unconditional worth, dignity and adequacy.

2. Be yourself

Avoid hiding your true self behind an act, a role, or a mask, in order to conform to the expectations of others, especially people in authority, in order to win their acceptance.

3. Forget yourself

When the inner toothache of painful self-rejection is removed, then and only then will we feel free to be ourselves and to pay undistracted attention to the experience of other people.

Some Symptoms of Low Self-esteem

1. Feelings of inferiority and lack of self-confidence. While appearing outwardly cool, there is a real inner shyness.

2. Difficulty in trusting others because of a fear of rejection. As a result it is very difficult to reveal one's deepest feelings and secrets.

3. Difficulty in receiving and accepting praise and thanks. They are desired, but when they are offered, they are shrugged off in one way or another.

4. Difficulty in asking or accepting help from others. People with low self-esteem are often very generous. They find it hard to say "no", lest people think badly of them . But they are slow to ask for help. Deep down they don't think they are worth it.

5. Exaggerated fear of failure is another sign of a poor self-image. People with low self-esteem are often perfectionists. They feel they will win acceptance and love because of what they do, rather than for who they are. Sometimes they brag, trying to draw attention to their achievements in order to be esteemed. Tragically, bragging often has the opposite effect.

6. Feelings of jealousy and envy undermine relationships. The insecure person becomes jealous because she doesn't feel she can compete successfully for love and affection. The envious person feels threatened by the gifts and talents of others. In the light of the superiority of another he feels inferior.

7. A tendency to judge and condemn because people with low self-esteem are harsh on themselves due to their perfectionism. They can become critical, sarcastic, cynical, judging and condemning of others in an off-putting way.

8. Difficulty in asserting their needs and opinions in conflict situations. Rather than face the possibility of having to cope with another person's anger, people with low self-esteem opt in a passive way for peace at any price.

Effects of Low Self-esteem

There are four notable effects of low self-esteem:

1. Sexual difficulties of all kinds rooted, not in lust, but in the nagging anxiety that comes from a poor self-image.

2. Addictions are often the result of low self-esteem. The person over-indulges in drinking, eating, smoking, taking pills and drugs in order to deaden the inner pain of self-rejection.

3. Negative emotions and aggressive behaviour, due to insecurity and over-sensitivity. Hurts come easily and can quickly turn to an anger that is expressed in aggressive words and deeds.

4. A tendency to illness due to the fact that insecurity, anxiety and negative emotions lead to stress. As a result the body's defences are lowered and illness occurs. Sixty to seventy per cent of patients in hospitals are there for this reason.

How to Improve Self-esteem

There are two main ways:

1. Heartfelt self-disclosure
Our self-image will be improved when we can tell one other human being about our real selves, about our failures, secrets and fears. We will never feel truly accepted, understood and loved until we know we are loved as we really are and not as we pretend to be. We can talk to a trusted friend or confidant such as a priest or a counsellor. As we sense and feel their loving acceptance we will begin to accept and love ourselves as we are.

2. Focus in prayer on the unconditional love of God.
Imagine Jesus standing before you. He is looking at you. Notice that

he is looking at you with eyes filled with love and humility. Hear him say: "I love and accept you just as you are. You do not have to change to receive my love. You don't have to become better, or give up your faults and failings. Obviously I would want you to do so, But that's not a condition for receiving my love and acceptance. That you have already, before you change, even if you never decide to change at all. Do you believe me? Do you believe that I accept and love you as you are, and not as you could be, or should be, or may be some day? Ponder what I'm saying to you and tell me what you really feel."

2. EMOTIONAL SELF-AWARENESS

Plato wrote: "Self-knowledge would certainly be maintained by me to be the very essence of knowledge, and in this I agree with him who dedicated the inscription, 'Know thyself!' at Delphi." Shakespeare advised: "This above all: to thine own self be true, and it must follow, as the night the day, thou canst not then be false to any man." Finally, Thomas a Kempis wrote in *The Imitation of Christ:* "The humble knowledge of yourself is a surer way to God than the deepest search after science."

Self-awareness is important for a number of reasons:

1. If people are unaware of their feelings, they will resemble brains on stilts, consciously rational, while often being influenced by unconscious feelings and prejudices. As St Francis de Sales reminds us: "Self-love is cunning, it pushes and insinuates itself into everything, while making us believe it is not there at all."

2. The quality of interpersonal relationships depends to a considerable extent on people's ability to reveal their feelings to others. However, they can only do this to the extent that they are aware of their emotions.

3. If prayer is to be more than telling lies to God, people need to reveal their deepest feelings to the Lord. This isn't possible for those who are out of touch with their inner selves.

Self-knowledge and self-awareness

There are many people who fail to distinguish between self-knowledge and self-awareness. The former is knowledge *about* the self. It can be acquired by reading psychology books, doing personality tests e.g. the Enneagram and the Myers Briggs Personality Type Indicator. It doesn't necessarily lead an increased awareness of one's subjective state. Self-awareness, however, is direct awareness *of* one's subjectivity, i.e. of inner emotions, moods, desires, reactions etc. It can be articulated afterwards in conceptual terms as self-knowledge.

Feelings are the fingerprints of subjectivity, similar to those of other people, but nevertheless unique. They put us in touch with two realities, the *external* world in which we live, and our own *inner* world, conditioned as it is by personal memories and influences of all kinds. We cannot will ourselves to feel anything e.g. to be joyful or sad. Feelings in fact are evoked by our perception of reality. As such they are revelatory because they tell us what we *really* perceive, value, or believe as opposed to what we *imagine* we perceive, value or believe. In that sense they never lie. If there is anything awry with our feelings it is because there is something awry with the way we look at the world and ourselves.

Five Steps to Emotional Self-awareness

1. Notice what you feel.
There are a number of ways of doing this.
(a) It is necessary to arrange appointments with yourself by taking time out to get in touch with your experience.

(b) If you are tense, you will find that you feel numb inside, so it is important to relax. As you do, the mists of anxiety will rise to reveal the inner landscape of feeling with its different emotions. For a number of relaxation exercises see Section 5, of this chapter *"Overcoming Stress"*.

(c) Take notice of your physical state. Is your mouth dry? Are your muscles aching? Have you a headache? Are you perspiring? Communicate with your body, asking it to translate its states into emotions. They may articulate themselves by means of images e.g. a memory of a violent scene on T.V. could be an indication of anger or fear.

In this connection, it is worth noting that remembered dreams can be helpful. The unconscious mind uses these night-time videos to express our deepest but neglected feelings. For more on this subject, see "A Christian Understanding of Dreams".

2. Naming feelings

Many of us are emotionally illiterate. When asked what we feel, all we can reply is that we feel "good", or "bad", as the case may be. Psychologists say that there are about eight primary emotions – surprise, fear, disgust, anger, happiness, sadness, expectancy and acceptance. So ask yourself, which of these emotions most resembles your own? Of course the primary emotions have many relatives. For example, under the heading of fear, we could include alarm, dread, apprehension, consternation, dismay, terror, fright, panic, trepidation etc. If possible try to describe your feelings in a more accurate and nuanced way. It takes time and effort to get good at this.

3. Owning feelings

Self-knowledge is inclined to say in an objective way, "I know that there is anger inside me." The person knows it is there, but he or she keeps it at arm's length. We own our feelings when we stop thinking about them, to become directly aware of their content. It is then that one can say, for example, "I feel really angry about the way in which I was cheated."

4. Understanding feelings

Albert Ellis has shown how the way we feel is conditioned by our perception of people and events. Our perceptions are influenced by a unique blend of our past experiences, and our personal beliefs, values and interests. So when we want to understand a feeling we can ask ourselves the following questions.

(a) What perception, value or belief evoked my feeling? For example, why did I feel afraid when I was licked by a neighbour's dog? Is it because I believe that, as an irrational creature, a dog is not to be trusted, as he could attack and cause me an injury?

(b) What in my earlier life might have conditioned the way I perceive things? For example, I may be afraid of dogs either because one of them attacked me when I was young, or because a dog bit someone I knew.

(c) Is my way of perceiving things, really realistic or for that matter Christian? For example, are all dogs really wild and aggressive? Surely not. Implicit in this realisation is the invitation to change my attitude to dogs.

5. Expressing feelings

Aristotle is reputed to have said: "There is nothing impressed which is not expressed." We can express our feelings in a number of ways.

(a) By "journalling" i.e. not only recording daily events in a diary, but also one's feelings about them, and one's insight into those feelings.

(b) By expressing them to a friend, confidant, counsellor, or spiritual director.

(c) By expressing them to God in private prayer. For more on this see "Prayer as Friendship with God".

Conclusion

While it is true that knowledge of objective truth is more important than subjective feelings, nevertheless, feelings are important. They add colour and energy to our relationship to reality. As Bernard Lonergan, one of the great philosophers of the century, has pointed out, it is much better to to take notice of one's feelings, however deplorable they may be, than to brush them aside, overrule them, ignore them. To take notice of them makes it possible for one to know oneself, to uncover the inattention, silliness, or irresponsibility that gave rise to the feeling one does not want and to correct a mistaken value, attitude or belief. As such, feelings play a vital role in the process of becoming at once more human and more Christian.

3. A CHRISTIAN UNDERSTANDING OF DREAMS

The Science of Dreams

We spend about a third of our lives sleeping. A fifth of that time is spent in dreaming. Thus, every twenty years or so, we spend one year in dreamland. That said, we only remember about five per cent of our dreams. Freud thought that the majority of them give expression to erotic wishes. Jung's approach was different. While he accepted that some dreams were sexual, he felt that others gave expression to deep-seated spiritual desires for wholeness and meaning. Unlike Freud, who thought that religious desires were a form of neurosis, Jung thought that neurosis was probable without them.

Dreams in the Bible and Christianity

1. The Old Testament: In the Old Testament, dreams were called the "dark speech of the Spirit".In the book of Job we read: "God speaks again and again in dreams, in visions of the night, when sleep falls on men as they lie on their beds. He opens their ears at times like that and gives wisdom and instruction." (33:14).

2. The New Testament: Dreams play an important role in the New Testament. In Matthew's gospel we see how St. Joseph had no less than four religious dreams. They all had to do with the birth and protection of Jesus. Near the end of the same gospel, we read how God the Father tried to protect his beloved Son from suffering by means of the inspired dream of Pilate's wife. In the Acts of the Apostles there are many examples of religious dreams. For example, St. Paul came to Europe as a result of one (16:14-16).

3. Dreams in Christian history: Tertullian stated a common point of view in early Christianity, when he said: "Is it not known to all people that the dream is the most usual way that God reveals himself to man?" Many momentous changes took place in Christian history as a result of inspired dreams. The Roman Empire ceased to be pagan as a result of a religious dream experienced by emperor Constantine. St. Patrick came to Ireland after a dream which he recounted in his "Confessions". That was in the fifth century. Since then, many holy men and women have reported how God revealed himself to them in dreams. Of one such dream, St. Therese of Lisieux wrote: "I cannot express the joy of my soul since these things are experienced, but cannot be put into words. Several months have passed since this sweet dream, and yet the memory it has left in my soul has lost nothing of its freshness and heavenly charms."

Having and Interpreting Dreams
The following suggestions will help you to dream, and to interpret your dreams:

1. Before falling asleep at night, befriend your unconscious and ask God to give you a helpful dream.

2. As soon as you wake up, *recall* and *record* your dream. You can do this by telling someone else about it, by writing it down, or by speaking it into your tape recorder.

3. Use the following simple method of interpretation:
(a) *Title:* If your dream were a video, what would you call it?
(b) *Theme:* What is the main gist of your dream? If it were a video what would you say it is about?
(c) *Feeling:* What is the main emotion in the dream – fear, joy, relief, guilt, love, etc? This is the key to dream interpretation.
(d) *Issue:* What is the dream trying to bring to your attention? What is the unconscious trying to say to your conscious mind?

4. What recent event, emotional conflict, or feeling may have prompted the dream? For example,

(a) When did I feel that way during the past few days?

(b) What was it about the remembered incident that evoked my feeling or reaction?

(c) Has that feeling any emotional roots in the distant past e.g. a traumatic experience?

(d) Does my dream cast any light on how to react in similar situations in the future?

5. Learn to interpret the *symbolism* in dreams. For example, water can be a symbol of life, death, purification, the unconscious, infinity, etc. The context of the symbol in the dream will usually act as the key to its meaning. Reputable books on dream symbolism can be useful in this regard, e.g. T. Chetwynds' *A Dictionary For Dreamers* and *A Dictionary of Symbol,* published by Paladin.

6. See the people and places in the dream as personifications of different aspects of the personality. Jung wrote: "The dream is the theatre of the mind where the dreamer is at once scene, actor, prompter, stage manager, author, audience and critic." A woman's dream about her own death and funeral might be interpreted in a literal way as a premonition of her impending death; from a metaphorical, and symbolic, point of view it could be seen as a dramatization of the woman's fear of life and a tendency to withdraw from its demands.

7. Occasionally a person may be granted an inspired dream about future events e.g. St. Joseph in Matthew's gospel. But by and large the Father wants us to leave the future in his hands and to trust him one day at a time .

The Discernment of Dreams
Dreams, like any other kind of inspiration, need discernment to see if they come from the Lord or not. The following questions can be useful in this regard:

1. Does the dream tend to move me into deeper relationship with God?

2. Does the dream help me to accept myself, to be myself, and to forget myself in outgoing love of others?

3. Does the dream evoke feelings of consolation e.g. joy, peace, hope etc. or of desolation e.g. sadness, restlessness, lack of hope, anxiety, etc? Consolation comes from God, desolation does not.

4. Does the dream help me to resist temptation and to embrace God's will of love out of conviction?

Conclusion
It has been said that dreams are letters from the unconscious. Some are written by the Spirit in the chamber of the heart, on paper supplied by the imagination. These letters need to be opened and read, as messages from God. They can heal the rift between the conscious and the unconscious mind. Religious dreams can lead us into self-knowledge and into an experiential knowledge of God. They can also energize more satisfying forms of personal prayer insofar as they reveal issues and feelings that can be shared with the Lord in loving communication. Finally, dreaming can help us to discover what we really desire. The Dreamer within, i.e. the Holy Spirit, fills us with holy longings for the coming of God's Kingdom. These longings will only be fulfilled when we wake from the final sleep of death, to behold the Lord, no longer as in a dream, but face to face.

4. SUFFERING T.H.E. CHRISTIAN WAY

The Experience of Suffering
Life isn't easy. Sufferings come to all of us. Perhaps the most common kinds are:

1. Negative Emotional States such as loss, grief, fear, resentment, insecurity, depression etc.

2. *Addiction* to things like alcohol, gambling, sleeping pills, tranquillisers, drugs, inappropriate forms of sexual satisfaction etc.

3. *Sickness, Injury or Handicap* which continues to cause trouble despite the best efforts of the medical profession.

A Key Question
In spite of all their efforts, philosophers, theologians and psychologists are unable to produce a satisfactory, rational explanation of why people have to suffer.

Where suffering is concerned, there is only one question worth asking: *Will it make you bitter or better?*

It will make you better if you learn to cope with it in a Christian way.

T.H.E. Christian Way of Suffering
There is a three step approach to suffering in the New Testament. It can be called T.H.E. Christian way.

1. **T** Thank God in the midst of suffering.
2. **H** Hand your suffering to God.
3. **E** Expect God to either help or to heal you.

Thank God No Matter What Happens
In (1 Thess. 5:18) St. Paul writes these words: "Give thanks *in all circumstances* , for this is God's will for you in Christ Jesus." Again in Eph 5:20, we read: "*Always* and *everywhere give thanks* to God who is our Father in the name of our Lord Jesus Christ." Finally in Col 3:17 we read: "*Always be thankful*....Whatever you say or do, let it be in the name of the Lord Jesus, in thanksgiving to God the Father through Christ." We can even thank God while we suffer. We believe that He has allowed our misfortune for a purpose. In the words of the Easter Liturgy, it is a "happy fault". God will bring blessings from our hurt. So try to do the following:

1. Call to mind your greatest suffering.

2. Tell God what you really feel about it e.g. anger, discouragement etc.

3. Now express your faith conviction by thanking God for your suffering in so far as you believe that there is a treasure of grace hidden in the field of your pain.

Hand Your Suffering to the Lord

Corrie Ten Boon, a survivor of a concentration camp, wrote these striking words: *"Nestle in the Lord, don't wrestle with your suffering."* In other words, nestle in the Lord through faith, rather than wrestling with your suffering in a self-absorbed way. This echoes what St. Peter said (1 Pt. 5:7): "Cast your anxieties on the Lord, for he cares about you." So try to do the following:

1. See Jesus on the cross and ponder these words: "Surely he took up our infirmities and carried our sorrows" (Is. 53:4).
2. Consciously offer your suffering to Jesus.
3. Tell the Lord that you trust him.

Expect God to Help or Heal You

The Lord says: "Blessed are those who mourn for they shall be comforted" (Mt. 5:4). He fulfils his promise in two main ways:

(a) He helps people to bear their suffering with patience and even cheerfullness. He uses it to:
  - purify the personality. "The Lord has led you in the wilderness, in order to humble you, testing you to know what was in your heart." Deut 8:2-3.
  - enable growth in self-knowledge. As Jung said: "There is no growth in consciousness without suffering."
  - develop character. "Suffering produces endurance, and endurance produces character, and character produces hope." Rm 5:4.
  - teach compassion. "The God of all comfort, comforts us in all our affliction, so that we may be able to comfort those who are in any affliction, with the comfort with which we ourselves are comforted by God." 2 Cor 1:4.

- enable people to share in the sufferings of Christ. "I rejoice in my sufferings . . . I complete what is lacking in Christ's afflictions for the sake of his body the Church." Col 1:24.

(b) God can prompt an inner desire for either physical, emotional or spiritual healing. When He does, do the following:

1. Consider these words about the passion of Jesus (Is. *53:5): "By his wounds our wounds are healed."*

2. Ask God to heal you with the kind of faith that expects results knowing that *"nothing is impossible to God"*. (Lk. 1:37).

3. Thank God in anticipation of the healing He is giving you. The seeds of that healing are being planted. They will bear fruit in the future.

A Final Prayer
Lord, I accept my sufferings. I thank You that You will bring a blessing from them. I give them to You in the confident expectation that You will help or heal me in accordance with Your loving plan for my life, through Christ our Lord. Amen.

5. OVERCOMING STRESS

The Nature and Effects of Stress
Nature has equipped us to cope with danger. In an emergency situation the body goes on red-alert. The brain automatically triggers a number of physiological changes. Adrenalin is produced. Digestion slows. Breathing gets faster. The heart rate accelerates. Blood pressure rises. Perspiration increases. Sugar and fat are secreted. They provide the body with extra energy. Muscles grow tense, ready for "flight or fight". Brief bouts of this kind of stress can be helpful in life and death situations. They prepare us for appropriate action. While the pace and pressure of modern life can be hectic, they are

rarely life-threatening. Nevertheless, many of us react as if they were. As a result our stress levels may go up and remain high. This can have harmful physical and psychological effects.

Physical Effects of Unrelieved Stress

1. It can lead to problems such as high blood pressure, migraines, heart disease, strokes, ulcers, asthmatic conditions, cold hands and feet, flatulence, palpitations, etc.

2. It can aggravate conditions such as backache, arthritis, multiple sclerosis, allergies, hyperthyroidism, etc.

3. It weakens the body's defences against illnesses such as colds and flu, and diseases such as cancer.

It is estimated that at least sixty per cent of sickness is stress related.

Psychological Effects of Unrelieved Stress

1. The victim suffers from painful feelings of anxiety, fear and depression. He/she may experience panic attacks.

2. The victim finds it hard to cope with any pressure. His/her fuse is short. He/she gets angry and hostile.

3. Concentration slips. Mistakes are made. Mental blocks occur. Sleep patterns are disturbed. There are many bad dreams. The person gets up feeling tired and tense.

4. The victim tries to escape from stress by eating, drinking or smoking too much. He or she may suffer from some kind of sexual problem e.g. impotence.

5. The victim may suffer from "burn-out". It is not a nervous breakdown but rather a state of extreme physical and emotional exhaustion.

Not surprisingly, unrelieved stress can effect a person's spiritual life. He/she becomes defensive, introverted, and self-absorbed. His/her prayer becomes distracted. God may seem to be distant and unreal. Instead of peace, there can be agitation and disturbance in the heart.

Means of Overcoming Stress

It is important that you believe that stress *can* and *should* be managed, because there are outer environmental and inner physical causes of stress. You have to tackle both.

Changes in Life Style

1. Establish priorities

It is important to discriminate between *needs* and *priorities*. The president of an American steel company told a New York management consultant. "I'll pay you any price if you will tell me how to get more things done, without undue stress." The consultant replied: "At night spend five minutes analysing your problems of the following day. Write them down on a sheet of paper, but place them in the order of their importance. Then tackle the first item as soon as you reach the office. Stick to it until it is finished. Then shift to number two, and so on. Test this method as long as you like. Then send me as much as you think it is worth." Some time later the consultant received $25,000, with a note: "This is the most practical lesson I have ever learned!"

Whether at home or at work you can use this method.

2. Keep fit

If adrenalin is building up in the body as a result of unrelieved stress, exercise will help to use it up. Not only that, you will be more resistant to stress when you are fit. Take some form of regular exercise. Set a realistic goal. Do something you will enjoy. The experts think that a brisk walk for up to an hour is best.

3. Diet

You should avoid using chemicals that cause stress such as caffeine, sugar, salt, and the like. If you are over-weight, try to begin a sensible diet. Two simple ways of doing this are, firstly, avoid eating between meals, and secondly, avoid sugar in all its forms e.g. chocolate and sweets, desserts, cakes, biscuits, etc. As you lose surplus pounds, your stress levels will go down, and your self-esteem will go up.

4. Take recreation

Don't live to work. Try to work in order to live. Recreation is a priority. Spend time tuning in to your feelings, needs, desires, etc. Meet with friends and share with them. Enjoy your hobbies. Not only are these forms of relaxation essential for a sense of well-being, but also they help to reduce stress levels.

Attitudinal Change

1. Use a relaxation exercise

According to medical experts, nothing helps to reduce stress more than an effective relaxation exercise. There are many of them. Try one of the following three.

(a) Breathing

Sit or lie quietly. Close your eyes. Imagine a tranquil scene e.g. wispy clouds in a blue sky on a summer's day. Breathe slowly and deeply, through your nose. Make each out-breath long and soft and steady. Sense the tension leave your body as you exhale.

(b) Physical Exercises

Sit or lie quietly. Close your eyes. Clench both fists for about 15 seconds. Then relax them and feel the tension draining away from your arms and muscles. Repeat this twice. Then hunch your shoulders for 15 seconds and relax, feeling the tension draining away. Continue the same method with jaw clenching and relaxing. And finally screw your eyes up tightly and relax them, feeling the tension disappear. Do the same with your legs etc.

(c) Focused attention
• Sit or lie in a comfortable position.
• Close your eyes and try to relax your muscles.

- Smile inwardly and with eyes and mouth.
- Try to breathe slowly and naturally.
- Select a religious word or phrase that means a lot to you, for example, "Fear not, I am with you." (Is. 41:10)
"The battle is not mine but yours, O Lord." (2 Chon. 20:15)
"As the Father loves me so I love you." (Jn. 15:9)
"The peace I desire is within."
"Maranatha, come Lord Jesus."

Repeat your chosen word or phrase as you exhale.

Try to focus your mind and imagination on the word or phrase. Avoid thinking about it.

When outside thoughts intrude during your meditation period quietly and gently disregard them saying: "Oh well!" and then return to your chosen word or phrase. It is essential to maintain a passive, relaxed style in dealing with any interruptions.

If this exercise is done for 20 minutes each day it will begin to have a very calming effect. As the mind's attention becomes focused and disciplined, the whole body relaxes. (For more on this exercise see *Beyond the Relaxation Response* by Herbert Benson, published by Fount Books).

2. Learn to cope with conflict

In relationships, conflict is inevitable. There are two stressful ways of handling your sense of hurt, frustration and anger.
- *Passively,* i.e. by burying your anger alive. It will attack you and cause anxiety and depressive feelings.
- *Aggressively,* i.e. by attacking the offender in word or deed. This usually evokes a counter-attack, and increased stress.
- The constructive way forward with family and friends especially, is to act *assertively.* Instead of repressing your feelings, or attacking the other person's, report your sense of hurt, anger or frustration e.g. "I felt hurt and angry, when you seemed to ignore my views at the meeting yesterday." Where your rights are concerned, be assertive also e.g. in a shop "The clock you sold me two days ago doesn't work properly, the alarm is broken. *I want a new clock.*" If the assistant is reluctant, don't argue, keep on asserting your rights: "*I want a new clock!*"

3. Be motivated by conviction not merely by obligation
Many people suffer from what has been called "hardening of the oughteries". They are motivated by the "musts, shoulds, oughts, and have-tos" of other people. This leads to feelings of stress. Get used to asking yourself. "What do I want, desire, need in this situation?" As you grow in inner freedom and autonomy, your stress levels will go down.

4. Improve your self-esteem
This is a big subject. See the chapter on this subject above. For a fuller treatment see "Self-Esteem and the Love of God" in my *Growing in Health and Grace,* published by Campus Publishing, Galway, 1991.

6. CRISES IN LIFE: OPPORTUNITIES FOR GROWTH

To Live Is to Change
Heraclitus wrote: "You cannot step into the same river twice, for other waters are ever flowing onto you." Cardinal Newman echoed this observation when he wrote: "To live is to change, and to be perfect is to have changed often."

Our bodies are constantly changing. In the space of seven years every cell within us is replaced!

Psychologically and spiritually we undergo change, especially during times of crisis. They are *the* turning points for better or for worse in our lives.

There are two main forms of crisis, *predictable* and *unpredictable*.

(a) *Predictable crises*: Developmental psychologists maintain that in every decade of our lives we can expect to face an inward crisis of three years duration. Its purpose is to urge us to tackle some developmental task, and so to grow into a new depth of maturity.

(b) *Unpredictable crises:* These occur when the "slings and arrows of outrageous fortune" come our way, e.g. the death of a close relative, a heart attack, cancer, etc. Often in life a predictable crisis will occur at the same time as one or two unpredictable ones.

These life crises have a discernible structure:

1. Onset and restlessness
2. Darkness and exploration
3. Resolution and re-stabilization

Let us look at the spiritual and psychological significance of these periods of transition in our lives.

Onset and restlessness
A woman may face a predictable crisis with the onset of the menopause. At the same time she may have to cope with the fact that her husband has lost his job and that her unmarried daughter has become pregnant. Like countless other people she begins a time of painful transition. She feels that she is losing control over her life. She enters a sort of "no man's land" where things happen to her. She feels like a victim. Troubling feelings begin to well up inside, such as anxiety, fear, guilt, confusion and mild depression.

Darkness and exploration
Times of crisis are often times of disillusionment. The ways we look at ourselves, others and God are challenged. Values and priorities that sustained us in the past seem inadequate now. Not surprisingly, we lose our inner sense of joy and peace. Instead we feel agitated and restless. God seems distant and unreal. Prayer is difficult while temptations are strong and frequent. What exactly is happening from a spiritual point of view? In Jer. 17:9-10 we read: "The heart is deceitful above all things and desperately corrupt, who can understand it? I the Lord, search the mind and try the heart."

The Lord does this by means of a transitional crisis. In this way the Lord helps us to carry out the teaching of St. Paul: "Do not model yourselves on the behaviour of the world around you, but let your behaviour change, moulded by your new mind." (Rm. 12:2).

Plaster models are made in rubber moulds. As a result they assume the shape of the mould. Unconsciously our sense of self and values can be moulded by the world. This secular or false self has a number of characteristics.

1. Its sense of worth is secretly dependent upon such things as success, reputation, status, etc.

2. It has a compulsive desire to acquire and defend these things, and a lurking fear of losing them.

3. It tends to reject any experience from either the outer or inner world which might threaten its sense of security or control. It does this by means of denial, projection, rationalization, etc.

4. People with a secular or false sense of self tend to identify with roles, e.g. housewife, priest, trade-unionist, etc. Apart from the role they often lack a personal sense of identity.

5. The false self often acts out of a sense of duty. It is motivated by words of obligation e.g. "I ought, must, should, have to" do such-and-such. It is less likely to be motivated by words of personal conviction e.g. "I want, desire, need, yearn to" and the like.

During a transitional crisis the Lord will often remove those things which have been sustaining our false, secular sense of self. Instead of enjoying success, status and a good reputation we may have to drink the bitter wine of failure, loss and humiliation. This could well be the case with the menopausal woman whose husband is unemployed and whose unmarried daughter is pregnant. As the scaffolding that once supported the false self is removed there is a painful sense of hurt and grief. This usually turns to the emotion of anger. Some people repress this feeling. As a result it attacks them, making them feel more insecure and depressed. God's presence seems remote and prayer unreal. It is healthier to get in touch with the anger and to admit it to oneself, to another and to God. As this is done three main things begin to happen.

1. We begin to get in touch with the roots of the anger. For example we may come to recognize that, although we felt we were keeping the first commandment by putting God number one in our lives, things like success, status, reputation etc. had become our real gods. In this way our sense of anger, fear, loss and anxiety, becomes a call to conversion.

2. As we come to terms with our anger and its causes during a time of crisis we usually get in touch with our deep down-desire for a new sense of God, self and values. This is what we call a "holy desire", one that is inspired by the Spirit and which prepares us for a new revelation of the Lord and his will.

3. As we pour out our feelings and our desires to the Lord, *chronos* i.e. "unredeemed time", gives way to *kairos* i.e. "sacred time", when the Lord reveals himself and his will to us. For example, during a period of difficulty one could be led to a scripture text such as Is. 41:10: "Fear not, I am with you, be not dismayed, for I am your God, I will strengthen you, I will help you, I will uphold you with my victorious right hand."

These words are comforting in the sense that they give a person the strength to battle on. Consolation comes later. It can come as a result of healing dreams and vivid experiences of the unconditional love of God. These can have the effect of re-focusing the personality. It begins to move away from secular values to become more centred on Christ and gospel values. In this way St. Paul's advice is fulfilled: "You must give up your old way of life, you must put aside your old self, which gets corrupted by following illusory desires. Your mind must be renewed by a spiritual revolution so that you can put on the new self that has been created in God's way." (Eph. 4:22-23).

Psychologists such as Jung and Erikson have shown that

psychological development takes place as a result of experiencing life crises. It is a matter of break-down leading to break-through. Old ways of looking at ourselves break down under the pressure of new challenges and as a result we have the opportunity of breaking through to new ways of seeing ourselves and our priorities, e.g. in early adulthood we tend to be extroverted and preoccupied with the external world. At mid-life the focus tends to change: we become more introverted and preoccupied with spiritual values and the journey inwards.

Resolution and Re-stabilisation

As we emerge from a transitional crisis with a matured sense of God, self and values, we appreciate what Jesus meant when he said that the grain of wheat has to die in order to grow and bear fruit, c.f. John 12:24.

Meister Eckhart once wrote: "A man has many skins in himself, covering the depths of his heart. Man knows so many things; he does not know himself. Why, thirty or forty skins or hides, just like an ox's or a bear's so thick and hard cover the soul. Go within and learn to know yourself there."

Transitional crises are God's invitation to do just that.

7. HEALTHY AND UNHEALTHY FORMS OF GUILT

It is important that Christians learn to distinguish healthy from unhealthy guilt: one is truly spiritual, the other neurotic in nature. Although Freud was an unbeliever, he has helped us to understand this difficult area.

Freud's Description of Personality

Freud's theory of personality is based on a conflict between what he called the Id, the Ego and the Superego.

1. *The Id* is the seat of the instincts and drives which are guided by the pleasure principle, e.g. a need for sexual satisfaction. The Id is amoral, largely unconscious and partly revealed in dreams.

2. *The Ego* embraces the person's conscious self-awareness as it relates in a realistic way to outer and inner reality. It is orientated toward relationship, and values and beliefs which are accepted as a result of personal conviction.

3. *The Superego* represents the internalized values and attitudes of significant others, such as parents, carers, teachers and clergy. It manifests itself in the form of authoritative conscience.
• In its healthy form it helps to mediate traditional values.
• In its unhealthy form it is moralistic and overbearing, threatening to withdraw love and approval from the personality if it fails to live up to its impersonal demands and ideals.

How The Unhealthy Superego Develops
1. When a child is very small, it is totally helpless and totally dependent on its parents (or parental substitutes) for clothes, food and shelter.

2. The child is a bundle of undisciplined and selfish needs and desires. In an effort to socialize the child, its parents have to discipline it. They may give the child the impression in verbal and non-verbal ways that they will love it more *if* it behaves . . . *if* it doesn't urinate on the carpet . . . *if* it doesn't put jam on the wallpaper . . . *if* it doesn't cry too much, etc. Although the child desires to do its "own thing", it desires the apparently conditional love of its parents even more. So it learns to conform in order to retain their affection and acceptance.

3. As the child develops, it begins to internalize the values and attitudes of its parents, in the form of conscience. This is what Freud refered to as the superego. Its demands often become synonymous with the demands of God. As a result, if either the growing child or

an adult indulges in any forbidden instinctual behaviour, e.g. of a sexual kind, the unhealthy superego may say, "Because you did a bad thing, you are a bad person, you can no longer love or accept yourself, and the same is true of God, He doesn't love or accept you either."

Symptoms of an Unhealthy Superego

1. It is conformist and perfectionist in its outlook. It is motivated by external authority, the expectations of others, and expresses itself in the language of obligation, e.g. I must, I ought, I have to, I should. The personality hasn't much inner authority. It rarely expresses itself in the language of conviction e.g. I need, I desire, I believe, I want, etc.

2. People with unhealthy superegos tend to be critical, judgemental and condemnatory in their thoughts and words. They treat others as badly as they already treat themselves. They are inclined to project their guilt on to others by seeing the splinter in their neighbour's eye while failing to acknowledge the plank in their own.

3. Whenever they fail to live up to their idealistic standards, they not only feel that they are bad and unlovable, they can suffer from remorse, alienation, isolation, anxiety and mild depression. Ironically, these negative feelings arouse instinctual desires, often of a sexual kind, as a way of revitalizing their personalities. One psychologist has suggested that 85% of our sexual fantasies and deeds are rooted in such negative inward states rather than in lust. However, if the person happens to offend against the dictates of conscience, he or she experiences even greater anxiety, and so a vicious circle is completed.

4. Instead of seeing sin in terms of relationship, as a failure to respond to the unconditional love of God, people with superego problems see it in terms of impersonal moral principles, as a failure to keep the law.

5. They are sorry for their sins, not because they withdrew their love from God, but because they are afraid that God has withdrawn His apparently conditional love from them.

6. If they go to confession, they do so in order to placate the God of harsh justice and to win back His love and approval. They invest their faith in the way in which they confess their sins, i.e. in their number and kind, rather than in the loving mercy of God. Not surprisingly, many of them tend to be scrupulous.

7. When they receive absolution they experience relief rather than real peace. They get back to square one but there is no real growth in their relationship with God. As a result, they may have the desire to do better in the future, but they don't have the power to do so. Despite their purpose of amendment, they will tend to repeat the same sins and confessions, time and time again.

How to Overcome an Unhealthy Superego
1. Try to become aware of the activity of the unhealthy superego in your life.

2. Avoid asking what you *ought* to do. In the light of your relationship with the Lord and with other people ask yourself what it is that you would *want* to do.

3. In prayer focus on the *unconditional* love of God. For more on this see, "Self-esteem and the love of God," above.

4. Try to see moral values in terms of conscious relationship with God, rather than in terms of abstract laws.

5. If you are going to confession, ask the God who searches every heart to search yours to help you to know your sin i.e. the areas in your life where you failed to respond to the unconditional love He has shown you.

6. Ask the Lord for the grace of perfect contrition, i.e. feeling sorry

for your sins, not because you have a morbid and mistaken fear that God has withdrawn His conditional love from you, but because you have selfishly withdrawn your love from the Lord.

7. In prayer meditate upon one or more of the following texts.
(a) Lk 15:11-32: the story of the prodigal son.
   • The younger son who indulges his desires without restraint represents the id.
   • The father who is compassionate, accepting, understanding and generous represents the Christian ego.
   • The elder brother who is dutiful, judgemental and harsh represents the superego.
(b) Lk 7:35-50: the story of the woman who washed the feet of Jesus.
   • Mary, the prostitute who indulged the desires of the flesh, represents the id.
   • Jesus in his love, understanding and disregard of public opinion represents the Christian ego.
   • Simon, the pharisee who is impersonal, critical and moralistic represents the unhealthy superego.
(c) Lk 18:9-15: the pharisee and the tax collector.
   • The tax collector, who is dishonest and disloyal, symbolises the id.
   • Jesus, who is discerning and compassionate, is like the Christian ego.
   • The pharisee, who is proud, dutiful, judgemental and self-righteous, represents the unhealthy superego.

8. In Gal 5:1, St Paul writes: "For freedom Christ has set us free. Stand firm, therefore, and do not submit again to the yoke of slavery . . . The whole law is summed up in a single commandment, 'You shall love your neighbour as yourself'. Pray for a spirit of love and the freedom of the children of God."

PART TWO

You

1. I BELIEVE IN LOVE: A CREED

Some time ago I asked myself what I really believed. After a lot of reflection, I became aware of the fact that I believed unreservedly in the reality of love. Then one day, when I had a good deal of free time, I sat down and wrote this personal creed. Read it and see if you can share my beliefs. Perhaps, at some future date, you will write your own personal creed. It is a revealing and worthwhile thing to do.

I believe in love.
I believe that love is the ultimate reality.
I believe that Divine Love is uncreated and inexhaustible.
I believe that Divine creativity is the expression of love.
I believe that all created things have their origin in love.
I believe that all that exists is sustained in being by love.
I believe that creation finds its fulfilment in and through love.

I believe that a person's inner value can only be revealed to the look
of love.
I believe that love affirms the worth of the person it knows.
I believe that love uncovers the hidden potential of a person.
I believe that love enables that which it uncovers, to blossom and
thrive.
I believe that love is not motivated by a desire for advantages or
pleasures of any kind.
I believe that these benefits can follow as a consequence rather than a
motive of love.

I believe that this love became manifest in the person of Jesus Christ.
I believe that Jesus is the Son of God, who enjoys the love and
favour of the Father.
I believe that the Father sees and loves in each baptised person what
He sees and loves in His Son.
I believe that Jesus loves each person the way the Father loves him.
I believe that the Kingdom he proclaimed in words and demonstrated
in deeds is the reign of Divine Love.

I believe that the saving death of Jesus on the cross was the supreme
   expression of his love.
I believe that the Holy Spirit can lead a person into an inner
   awareness of God's love.

I believe that I am loved unconditionally by God.
I believe that this love cannot be earned or deserved.
I believe that this love is impressed upon the heart by being
   expressed in loving words and deeds.
I believe that the desire to love and be loved is the deepest yearning
   of the human heart.
I believe that we are empowered to love by the Holy Spirit.

I believe that true love is without condition.
I believe that such love is devoid of judgement or condemnation.
I believe that love is accepting and understanding.
I believe that love is kind-hearted, tender and compassionate.
I believe that love forgives all wrongs.
I believe that there is no pretence or bitterness in love.
I believe that love is the source of all comfort and consolation.
I believe that love seeks to unite those things that properly belong
   together.
I believe that love seeks to reconcile those who have become
   alienated from one another.
I believe that authentic relationships are the expression of love.
I believe that love is the spiritual milk of childhood.
I believe that love is the real meaning of sexual intimacy.
I believe that love is the true bond of friendship.
I believe that love transforms social union into the mystical presence
   of Christ.

I believe that anything alien to love is evil.
I believe that the presence of evil is discerned in the light of love.
I believe that love is stronger than evil.
I believe that love delivers us from all evil.
I believe that there is nothing negative in love.

I believe that love has the power to heal body, mind and soul.
I believe that love is the purpose and fulfilment of human freedom.

I believe that love is the fulfilment of all law and morality.
I believe that love is the ultimate justification and explanation of all things.
I believe that love itself is beyond justification or explanation.

I believe that the Eucharist is the sign, origin, and focus of Christian love on earth .
I believe that worship is the heart's graced response to the conscious awareness of the love of God and the God of love.
I believe that the resurrection of the dead will inaugurate the final triumph of love.
I believe that on the day of judgement we will be examined in love alone.
I believe that heaven is a state or place where Divine Love will transfigure all things.
Amen.

2. FRIENDSHIP LOVE

The Importance of Friendship
The English word "friend" comes from the Anglo-Saxon, meaning "to love". This kind of disinterested love can lead to a deep union of mind and heart. Not surprisingly, friendship was highly valued in the ancient world.

1. The Greeks and Romans had things like this to say about it:
• "A friend is a second self." (Pythagoras)
• "Friendship is one soul dwelling in two bodies." (Aristotle)
• "Friendship is the noblest and most delightful of all the gifts the gods have given to mankind." (Cicero)

2. The Old and New Testaments prize and encourage friendship.
• "A faithful friend is a sure shelter, whoever finds one has found a treasure. A faithful friend is something beyond price, there is no measuring his worth. A faithful friend is the elixir of life, and those who fear the Lord will find one." (Sir. 6:14-15)
• Jesus said: "I call you friends . . . Love one-another as I have loved you" (Jn. 15:14, 12)
• "The community of believers was one in mind and heart," says St. Luke in Acts 4:32; in other words they were a community of friends.

Ten Ingredients of True Friendship
When we read what the ancient and modern writers say about friendship, we can summarize their teaching under ten headings:

1. Equality: Despite differences in sex, age, education, etc. friends are attracted to one-another as equals, people whose mutual acceptance is based on the fact that they share many attractive qualities, values and interests in common.

2. Goodwill: Genuine friendship is not based on a self-centred desire for *advantage* or *pleasure*. It is more interested in promoting the growth and welfare of the friend than it is in satisfying its own needs.
3.Trust: If friendship is to grow it has to be based on the firm conviction that there is no reason to fear betrayal or exploitation of any kind. This kind of trust is evoked by the awareness of being accepted, appreciated and loved.

4. Loyalty: Potential friends need a probation period during which they try to find out if they have the qualities and motives for a genuine long-lasting relationship. If they think they have, they make a declaration of friendship, affection and mutual loyalty.

5. Forgiveness: Even the best of friends will hurt each other. Whether as a result of weakness or of malice, they will say or do things that they later come to regret. A willingness to forgive and to ask for forgiveness helps the friends to maintain and even deepen their relationship.

6. Respect: Friends refrain from asking each other to do anything that would clash with their values. Where values do come into conflict e.g. about the physical expression of affection between male and female friends, the stricter conscience should rule.

7. Self-disclosure: The ability to reveal one's real self is what makes friendship different from other relationships. "A friend," says St. Aelred of Rievaulx, "shares *all* the innermost secrets of your heart . . . to him you confide *everything* as if he were your other self." This is so because the impulse of friendship is to give. The greatest gift we can give to a friend is the gift of our real self. We never feel truly loved and accepted until we know that our friend knows and loves us as we are. Not only that, such disclosure of our deepest thoughts, feelings, and vulnerabilities, invites our friend to do the same. When he does we are receptive, able to attend to his sharing with openness.

8. Listening with empathy: Friends break free of the gravitational pull of self absorption.They listen not only to ideas and facts, but to feelings and experience as well. Friends try to forget their own concerns to become absorbed by those of the friend.

9. Confidentiality: Friends keep secrets. They know that there is nothing worse than hearing an acquaintance recounting a secret shared in confidence. It seriously undermines the trust upon which friendships are built.

10. Correction: All of us are blind to our own faults to a certain extent. Because they know this, friends accept correction in a spirit of trust and affection. They speak the truth in love, knowing that truth without love is cruelty while love without the truth is sentimentality.

Five Effects of Friendship
1. Friendship increases happiness: It has the effect of doubling joys and lessening sorrows. Friends enjoy each other's company,

conversation and activities. Aristotle went so far as to say: "Without friends, no one would choose to live."

2. Friendship heals: In Anglo-Saxon the words "friend" and "free" were closely related. When friendship-love is genuine, it provides a climate of emotional safety which enables friends to let go of their roles and masks, and to become their real selves. As they do so they come to terms with the darker, hurting side of their natures. Within the bonds of love and mutual acceptance they learn to have compassion on the rejected and weaker sides of their own natures. As a result self-esteem grows, anxiety diminishes, and the person is freer to go out to others in love.

3. Friendship enlightens: We learn a lot from friends, from what they say and from their example. Because they know us so well, and want what is best for us, friends are in a position to give us good advice when it is asked for.

4. Friendship leads to God: As they offer one-another the gift of love and acceptance, friends become for each other images of the presence of Jesus, The Friend. As they share their affection in a committed way, there may be precious moments. Their separateness may give way to a feeling that their personalities have become united in the awareness of God. In this way they come to experience the truth of the words of Jesus: "Where two or three come together in my name, there I am with them." (Matt. 18:20.) As a result St. Aelred could say: "God is friendship. It does sound strange, doesn't it? But I would not hesitate to attribute to friendship anything attributed to charity e.g. he who abides in friendship, abides in God and God in him."

5. Prayer is friendship with God: The experience of friendship is the key to understanding Christian prayer. In Ex. 33:7-12 we read about the prayer of Moses: "The Lord would speak to Moses face to face, as a man speaks with his friend." St.Thomas Aquinas wrote: "For friends to talk together is the natural thing for them to do. Men's conversation with God is through prayer of an attentive kind." For more on this see "Prayer as Friendship with God," below.

Conclusion

St. Francis de Sales has written: "Friends love one-another, they know they love one-another, and they have communication, intimacy and familiarity with one-another. O God! how precious this friendship is. It is excellent because it comes from God. Excellent because it leads to God. Excellent because its very bond is God. Excellent because it will last eternally in God. Oh, how good it is to love God on earth as they love in heaven, to learn to cherish one-another in this world as we shall do eternally in the next."

3. THE ART OF LISTENING

The Importance of Listening
The art of listening is the key to three interrelated things.

1. Good communication.
2. Loving relationships.
3. Openness to the presence and the word of God.

Three Forms of Listening
Our attitude to *feelings* will determine the way in which we listen. There are three forms:
(a) Listening with Apathy
The focus is on *facts* and *ideas* rather than *feelings*. The aim is to give objective advice rather than understanding. A man admits to being lonely, depressed and guilty about his excessive drinking.The man who listens in an apathetic way asks: "How many pints do you drink each day?" When he is told the number he replies: "You are drinking too much, you should try to do something about it." The troubled drinker knows this already. The listener's lack of

understanding and acceptance will deepen his depression, leaving him more likely to drink again.

(b) Listening with Sympathy
Objectivity is abandoned altogether in order to *share* in the other person's feelings. For example, the sympathetic listener gets so depressed by the drinker's story that he joins him in a nearby pub. Together they try to drown their sorrows! To share in feelings in this way is to become part of the problem and it isn't really helpful.

(c) Listening with Empathy
Here the intention is to *recognize* what the other person feels, and to respond emotionally to those feelings, without having to share in them. When the person with empathy hears the drinker's story, he might respond: "I could feel a sense of tenderness welling up when I realize how isolated and hopeless you had been feeling." This kind of response helps the drinker. He feels accepted and understood. As a result he may feel less need to drink heavily.

Ten Listening Skills
1. Show interest in the person: We do this by giving people our undivided attention. Eye contact, sympathetic nods, and reassuring gestures can help.

2. Focus on feeling: In relationships feelings are more important than facts or ideas. If a woman has just buried her mother, her feelings of loss, grief, and hopelessness are more important to her than the location of the cemetery, the number of mourners, or weather on the day of the funeral.

3. Focus on emotional attitudes: Many of our feelings are changeable and short-lived. But we may have fairly constant emotional attitudes to certain things. For example, we may have a morbid fear of anything to do with death, or predictable feelings of mistrust when dealing with anyone in authority.

4. Reflect back the main feelings and attitudes: As we become aware of what another person feels, we reflect back those feelings, especially the strongest ones. Having heard the woman describe her grief after her mother's death, we might say: "You are really missing your mother since she died. You seem to feel angry with God for allowing her to suffer so much toward the end and for not hearing your many prayers on her behalf." This kind of response will help the grieving woman to feel understood, and to recognize clearly for herself what she really feels.

5. Be aware of your own feelings and attitudes: As we listen to people, their words will evoke in us all kinds of memories and feelings. The sharing of the grieving woman might remind us of our own mother's death some years before, or give rise to a fear about her death sometime in the future. Unless we recognize such feelings as they arise, they will distract our attention from the other person. Once we are aware of them, we can put them aside and recommit ourselves to the act of listening.

6. Talk as little as possible: The good listener says as little as possible. He confines himself to open-ended questions, and to the task of reflecting back feelings and attitudes. He avoids completing sentences, interjecting words, or interrupting the speaker.

7. Avoid talking about yourself: Sometimes what a person says reminds us of a memory of our own. Mention of a death may bring to mind a similar death in our own family. We may begin to listen to that emotion-filled memory. We say: "I know what you are going through, I went through the same thing two years ago," while going on to recount the details. Instead of listening to the other person, we are in effect, asking him or her to listen to us. While we may have the best of intentions in sharing like this, it isn't really helpful. It is self-absorbed. In any case no two people react in the same way to death. Everyone's experience is unique.

8. Avoid judgemental comments: People's deepest need is to feel accepted and understood as they are. It is only then that they will feel free to share their deepest experiences and feelings. Judgemental attitudes or words put paid to this.They can be conveyed in phrases like "you must . . . you should . . . you ought to . . . you will have to do such and such." By accepting people as they are, and not as we would like them to be, we help them to accept themselves. This is the only foundation upon which the *desire* and the *power* to change can be established.

9. Avoid controlling the agenda: Sometimes we listen with a hidden agenda of things we think are important. As a result we may tend to ignore what the speaker wants to share, by asking a lot of questions that come from our own minds, and not from the unfolding conversation.

10. Be sensitive to body language: Research has shown that well over fifty per cent of communication is non-verbal. A shrug, a smile, a nervous laugh, gestures, facial expressions, tone and pace of voice and body positions can speak volumes, revealing what a person feels.

Christian Listening
The art of listening is an essential aspect of Christian love.

(a) Our ability to listen to one another is linked to our ability to listen to God. It has been written: "Many people are looking for an ear that will listen. They do not find it among Christians because Christians are too busy talking when they should be listening. He who no longer listens to his brother will soon be no longer listening to God either."

(b) When we pay attention to what people say about their relationship with God, it can be very inspiring. As a result we may ourselves enter into a new awareness of the Presence and the word of God.

(c) The ability to listen to our neighbour whom we can see, is a preparation to listen to the word of the Lord we cannot see. This would be particularly true of the reading of the scriptures at the Eucharist. As Jesus said: "He who has ears let him hear." (Matthew 11:15.)

4. THE ANGRY CHRISTIAN

The Christian View of Anger

Anger is one of the commonest emotions we experience in life. Scripture makes it clear that in itself anger is neither right nor wrong. It is evaluated in terms of its use and effects. In (Gal. 5:20) St. Paul speaks of unrighteous anger, echoing what Jesus said in (Mt. 5:21): "Whoever is angry with his brother will be brought to trial." But clearly Paul thinks that there is a righteous form of anger as well. He writes: "Be angry but without sinning . . . if you are angry, do not let your anger lead you into sin, and don't stay angry all day, lest you give the devil a chance." (Eph. 4:26-28). So the scriptures draw a distinction between appropriate and inappropriate forms of anger: the former is constructive, the latter destructive. We will look at both from the point of view of modern psychology.

The Dynamics of Anger

Each one of us has physical, psychological and spiritual needs. Roberto Assagioli has suggested that there are six of them.

1. We have a need to preserve our lives.
2. We have sexual needs – a desire for completeness and intimacy.
3. We have a need for the security that comes from association with other people.
4. We need to affirm ourselves – to be appreciated, recognized and respected as much as we believe that we deserve.
5. We are curious with a need for knowledge of the unknown and mystery.
6. Spiritually we need a sense of meaning and some form of relationship with God.

When needs like these are satisfied we feel happy and fulfilled. When they are denied by people or events we feel a sense of loss and hurt. It is this feeling of deprivation that gives rise to our anger. As Francis Bacon wrote in his *Essays* "No man is angry that feels not himself hurt."

Destructive Anger
Anger can be turned against oneself or others in a damaging way.

Against oneself
Many people are reared in homes where anger is not accepted. So as
children they learn to suppress anger in order to retain the affection
and approval of their parents. As this kind of denial is repeated it
becomes second nature. By the time they reach adulthood some of
these people find it very hard to acknowledge any anger. They will
have the *emotion* in their bodies e.g. it will cause headaches and
stress, without experiencing any *feeling* of anger. It has been buried
alive in the unconscious. From there it attacks the person with two
main effects (a) It leads to vague feelings of guilt (b) Self-esteem is
lowered while feelings of inadequacy, anxiety and insecurity seem to
increase. If the anger is not acknowledged at this stage, it can turn to
depression. According to the World Health Organisation, depression,
or the "Blue Plague" as it has been called, is the number one illness
of the western world. In my experience a lot of it is rooted in
suppressed anger.

Anger against others
Many people can feel their anger. It is not suppressed. Rather it is
expressed in an *aggressive* way in the form of criticism, sarcasm,
cruel jokes, judgemental comments and even physical violence. In
this instance the angry person renounces all responsibility for his
resentful feelings. In effect he says: "It's all your fault, and I'll make
you pay for it!" Not only can this kind of irresponsible anger ruin
relationships, it can tear societies apart. We have only to think of
Northern Ireland to see the sad proof of this.

Constructive Anger
At this point we will look at the ways in which destructive forms of
anger can be handled in a constructive way.

1. In relation to oneself
When a person has got used to suppressing his or her anger, it is
important to *recover, name, own* and *express* this important feeling.

• It is *recovered* by first getting in touch with the initial experience of hurt or loss.

• It is named when we can go beyond saying "I feel bad" to being able to distinguish our anger from feelings like upset, irritation, or mild annoyance.

• It is *owned* when we can admit to ourselves, "I feel angry . . . when I think of the way I was mistreated . . . humiliated" etc.

• It is *expressed* when we can tell someone – the person who injured us, or a friend – about our hurt and anger. When this is done our sense of guilt or depression begins to lift.

Sometimes when we acknowledge our hurt and anger, we will see, from a Christian point of view, that they are invitations to repentance. For example, I may have desires that are unrealistic e.g. wanting everyone to like me, or inappropriate e.g. as a married man wanting a female friend to respond sexually to my advances. I could feel frustrated and angry if these desires were denied. But when I reflect on my feelings and their inward causes, I come to see my anger as something that reveals my need to change. I can tell God about my feelings while asking Him for forgiveness and the grace to live in accordance with his Word in the Scriptures.

2. *In relation to others*
The first step here, in the words of John Powell, is to "accept that while other people can *stimulate* my anger, the *causes* lie within." So I have to take responsibility for my anger, instead of projecting it on to others. When I do this, I have a number of options.

(a) To decide to *forgive* the person or persons who have hurt me. The sooner I do this the better. Scripture urges us not to let the sun go down on our anger.

(b) If I have expressed my anger in an aggressive, destructive way – regardless of whether my anger was justifiable or not – I should *ask for forgiveness*.

(c) I may feel let down by God e.g. as a result of a death or a misfortune in my family. Anger wells up. It is important that I try to express my feelings to God. If I don't do this because of resentment or a fear that He might strike me down with a flash of lightning, my relationship with the Lord will become formal. He will seem distant and unreal, no matter what prayers I might say. But if I see my anger as a prayer looking for a voice, then I can bring my hurts to the Lord in the expectation of receiving his comfort and/or healing.

(d) Instead of suppressing feelings of anger in an unhealthy way, or expressing them in an aggressive way, I can learn to express them constructively. Sometimes this won't be appropriate because of a lack of time or opportunity. But in the case of people who are near and dear to me, it is important that I assert my sense of worth by expressing my feelings. For example if a friend failed to keep an appointment I could say: "I felt hurt and and angry when you didn't show up last night as arranged. I really felt cheesed off, disappointed, let-down and taken for granted." This approach helps to clear the air. As William Blake wrote: "I was angry with my friend, I told my wrath, my wrath did end." This is better than suppressing the anger and pretending everything is O.K. As a result we begin to sulk, give the other person the silent treatment, or take it out on someone else. It is also better than *accusing* the other person in a resentful and judgemental way e.g. "You are completely unreliable. Your word means nothing. You don't give a damn about anybody!" This approach only makes a bad situation worse.

(e) Righteous anger about an injustice being done to another, especially a poor or powerless person, can give rise to an "indignant compassion" that expresses itself in *action* for *justice*.

5. FORGIVING THOSE WHO HURT US

The Experience of Hurt

We hurt one-another. Usually it's due to weakness rather than malice.

1. At home parents can hurt their children. Their ability to love may be weakened by an unhappy marriage, financial worries, or emotional problems. They may be unable to express physical affection, or say the words "I love you." Instead there can be hurtful comments and criticisms. So children can grow up insecure, with a poor self-image and ill-prepared to face the challenges of life.

2. At school the sense of hurt can be reinforced by a teacher or a bully who acts in a sarcastic or sadistic way.

3. In adult life hurts are inevitable. A spouse can be unfaithful. A friend can be disloyal or betray a confidence. A relative can try to cheat us out of money or property. People can say insensitive things that wound us deeply. In these and countless other ways we can be injured by life.

Hurt and Unforgiveness

Anger is usually the first reaction to hurt. It's a healthy response if it is short-lived. But sometimes we let the sun go down on our anger. We nurse it.We keep thinking about the hurt and the one who caused it. Bit by bit the anger festers. It turns into bitterness, resentment and even hate. We enter a state of unforgiveness, unable to really love or accept the person who hurt us. As a result the following things can happen.

1. We desire to avoid the person we resent.

2. If we do meet, we avoid eye contact or any display of affection.

3. We overlook the person's good points while dwelling on his or her faults, real and imaginary, in thought and conversation.

4. We may have a desire for revenge, an urge to make the resented person suffer.

5. We tend to blame others, especially parents, for adult problems of our own, for example, alcoholism.

Some Effects of Unforgiveness

The state of unforgiveness has many bad effects.

1. It can divide families, communities and whole societies.

2. It can lead to the kind of emotional stress that lowers the body's natural defences against illness and diseases such as cancer, arthritis, heart problems, etc.

3. It can quench the flame of grace within us. While the heart may have difficulty in receiving divine inspirations, it is wide open to the false, divisive and destructive inspirations of the Evil One.

Motives For Forgiving Those Who Hurt Us

There are many motives for forgiving those who hurt us.

1. As sinners we desperately need the mercy of God. He offers us this precious gift through his Divine Son, Jesus. He died and rose for us, so that our sins could be washed away.

2. Jesus warned that we will only experience the mercy of God if we are willing to forgive one-another. In Matt. 18:21-35 the master punishes the unforgiving servant with great severity. Then Jesus says: "This is how my heavenly Father will treat each of you unless you forgive your brother from your heart."

3. Jesus said that an unforgiving person is not fit to pray or worship until he or she has first been reconciled, Matt. 5:23-25.

4. If we bear a grudge against a person who has died, it is possible

that he or she may not be able to rest in peace until we forgive him/her.

A Method of Forgiveness

Firstly, if you do bear a grudge against someone living or dead, which of these three positions describes your state of mind?

1. "I won't forgive, the hurt is too great."
In that case recall the following words of Jesus: "Judge not and you will not be judged, condemn not and you will not be condemned. Forgive and you will be forgiven . . . The measure you give to others is the measure you yourself will receive." Luke 6:37.

2. "I can't forgive no matter how hard I try."
This is true. Remember the words of Shakespeare: "To err is human, to forgive Divine."

3. "I want to forgive with the help of God."
This miracle will be made possible by the grace of God. Just as the Holy Spirit falls on the bread and wine at the Eucharist, so the same Holy Spirit falls upon the person who wants to forgive, transforming desire into reality.

Secondly, we come to a practical method of forgiving prayer.

1. Close your eyes.

2. Imagine the person you want to forgive is standing in front of you.

3. See the person surrounded by the light of God's merciful love. Or see Jesus standing behind the person, his hands resting affectionately on his or her shoulders. Notice that he looks at the person with the same love and mercy he extends to you.

4. Now say the following prayer, or something like it:
". . . *(Name the person)* In the name of Our Lord, Jesus Christ, who

loves us and who has died for the forgiveness of our sins, I forgive you from the botttom of my heart for the hurt you have caused me. I release you, and call down the blessing and peace of God upon you and thank God that you are now forgiven. Amen."

The word *Amen* means "Let it be so, I believe it is accomplished." If we happen to meet the person we have forgiven, our hurt, resentful feelings may begin to bubble up again. It is vital that we affirm in faith that they have no real power. They are merely ghost pains from the past. In reality, we stand in the grace and power of forgiveness. As we do this, agitation will give way to peace. All bitterness forgotten, we will be able to act in a loving way.

Some hurts go so deep that they can't be forgiven easily or quickly. Like an onion that is being peeled, one layer of hurt only reveals another. And so forgiveness has to come in stages. Perhaps this was an implication in Jesus' saying that we should forgive "seventy times seven" (Mt 18:22) i.e. time and time again until the forgiveness is complete.

Effects of Forgiveness

Forgiveness brings many blessings.

1. Reconciliation in relationships.
2. An inner sense of freedom and joy.
3. A renewed sense of God and His inspirations.
4. Healing of mind and body, sometimes in a miraculous way.
5. An effective witness to the unconditional love of God.

Final Prayer
Father in heaven, take away my heart of stone, and give me a merciful heart like Yours. Forgive me for the many times I have hurt people. Help me in my turn, to forgive those who have hurt me, so that we may be united in the power of your love, through Christ our Lord. Amen.

6. CHRISTIAN COMPASSION

The Nature of Christian Compassion

Christian compassion is a sharing in the heart of God for wounded humanity, an experiential awareness of the love that Jesus felt for his suffering brothers and sisters.

(a) In the New Testament we are told on a number of occasions that the actions of Jesus were motivated by compassion e.g. although he was tired he preached to the people who had followed him into the wilderness because he had compassion on them because they were sad and dejected, like sheep without a shepherd. (cf Mk 6:34.)

(b) The quality of compassion was often highlighted in the parables of Jesus. For example, the prodigal father and the good Samaritan were motivated by this emotion. (cf Lk 10:33; 15:20)

In the Greek New Testement the word for "compassion" is *splangchnizomai.* The *splangchna* were the entrails or guts of the body. They were thought to be the source of people's most intense feelings and reactions. The word is related to the Hebrew word *rachamin* which refers to the womb. So it has been suggested that Christian compassion is a movement of the womb of God, one that seeks to give birth to new life in the suffering person who has evoked it. Author Henri Nouwen has written, "When Jesus was moved to compassion, the source of all life trembled, the ground of all love burst open, and the abyss of God's immense, inexhaustible, and unfathomable tenderness revealed itself."

Writing about Christian compassion, St Vincent de Paul wrote: "Another effect of charity is that it makes us unable to to see the neighbour suffer without suffering with him, to see him weep and not weep with him. Love makes people enter into the hearts and feelings of each other, they are different from those who feel no compassion for the afflicted or the suffering poor. Ah! but the Son of God was tender of heart. I cannot help constantly turning my eyes to this model of charity. He is called to visit Lazarus. He goes. Magdalen

57

rises and comes to meet him, weeping. The Jews follow and weep as well. What does the Lord do? He weeps with them. It was this tenderness of love that prompted him to come down from heaven. He saw that people were excluded from a share in his glory; he was touched by their misfortune."

From the point of view of psychology, compassion is the *empathy* we feel for those who suffer i.e. an ability to identify what another person feels, and to allow ourselves to spontaneously react to those feelings.

False Forms of Compassion

Compassion is not

(a) *Sympathy* i.e. a willingness to *participate* in the sufferings of the other person, e.g. becoming angry with the resentful, and depressed with the dejected.

(b) *Sentimentality* i.e. being in love with the idea of compassion and the feelings associated with it, without becoming involved with the person who is suffering. Tolstoy spoke of society women who would weep to see the sufferings of others as depicted in the theatre, while leaving their coachmen to wait in the freezing cold outside.

(c) *Repressed resentment:* people with suppressed feelings of inferiority and low self-esteem are inclined to have an unconscious sense of envy, anger and resentment against people that they consider to be rich, powerful or successful. As a result they tend to identify with the weak and the poor as fellow sufferers. Then in the name of compassion they judge and condemn the people they secretly admire.

(d) *Cheerless obligation:* compassion isn't something that I have to, or ought to express as a matter of Christian duty. Rather it is a matter of heartfelt conviction rooted in love.

Three Forms of Compassion
1. Compassion as fellow feeling: this is a kind of empathy which is

rooted in shared experience, e.g. the understanding that a member of Alcoholics Anonymous would have for a fellow addict.

2. *Wounded wonder:* even when we have no personal experience of a particular form of suffering e.g. alcoholism, we can have a deep sense of reverence and respect for the drinker's intrinsic worth and dignity. The extent to which he or she is wounded is the extent to which our sense of wonder is wounded also. There is no condescension in this kind of compassion. It affirms the sufferer's value and only in a secondary sense feels sorry for him or her.

3. *Indignant compassion:* as I sense the suffering of another person I may feel an anger which focuses on the causes of the suffering e.g. injustice, poverty, sickness etc. It is this kind of indignant compassion that enables me to feel united to the loving heart of Christ and that impels me to take appropriate remedial action, e.g. praying for healing, offering material assistance, changing unjust structures etc.

How to Grow in Compassion

There are a number of ways of growing in compassion.

(a) We can allow the predictable and unpredictable crises of life to challenge and to change those of our attitudes and values which are alien to compassion, for example, any that lead us to compete rather than to identify with people.

(b) To overcome our fear of suffering people e.g. travellers, handicapped children, social misfits, prisoners etc. By talking to them, hearing their stories and sensing what they feel, we will find that they will simultaneously evoke our respect and our compassion. I have found that as I befriend the weak and the wounded, I come to terms with the weakness and woundedness within myself.

(c) We can bring the feelings of compassion, which have been evoked by the sufferings of others, to the Lord in prayer. Then, as we seek His face, God can reveal Himself to us as the God of compassion, as the One who became poor for our sakes so that we might become rich in Him. As we come to appreciate the mind and heart of the Lord we will have a desire to be for others what He is for us i.e. compassionate and generous.

(d) If we are suffering ourselves, we can cast all our cares on the Lord, in the sure knowledge that He cares about us. He will comfort us in our sufferings, so that we may be able, in a spirit of compassion, to comfort others in their sufferings, with the very comfort that we ourselves have received from God.

Conclusion

Empathic listening is one of the principal ways of showing compassion to other people. For more on this see, "The Art of Listening," above. When it is appropriate and possible we can offer practical assistance. If we speak, we need to be sure that our words have firstly been dipped in the waters of compassion and cleansed of condescending pity or a holier-than-thou attitude of mind.

Compassion without action is sentimentality.
Action without compassion is condescension.
But compassion expressed in action is Emmanuel, God-with-us.

PART THREE

God

1. How to invite Jesus into your life

2. Be filled with the Spirit

3. The promises of God

4. Prayer as friendship with God

5. Reading and praying the scriptures

6. The power of petitionary prayer

7. The prayer of praise

8. Discerning the presence and power of God

9. Devotion to the Holy Spirit

1. HOW TO INVITE JESUS INTO YOUR LIFE

Restless For God

St. Augustine wrote: "You have made us for yourself, O Lord, and our hearts are restless until they rest in you."

We often experience that restlessness in the midst of crisis, disillusionment and suffering. Hidden desires well up. We begin to long inwardly for God. This yearning is Jesus knocking on the door of our hearts. He invites us in this way to lay to rest our restlessness in him. This is the key to Christian renewal. As Jesus assures us, "I am standing at the door knocking; if you hear my voice and open the door I will come in to you and eat with you and you with me." How do we open the door of our hearts in order to let Jesus into our lives? Well, imagine it is an Irish door, a DORAS. It has five planks:

> **D** for desire,
> **O** for offer,
> **R** for repent,
> **A** for ask, and
> **S** for submit.

Desire to Know Jesus

We need to be whole-hearted in our desire for Jesus. As the scripture says: "You will look for the Lord your God, and if you search for him with all your heart, you will find him." (Deut. 4:29) In Jer 29:12-14, we read: "When you call upon me and come and pray to me, I will hear you. When you search for me, you will find me, if you seek me with all your heart, I will let you find me, says the Lord, and I will restore your fortunes."

There is a story about a young man who came to St. Kevin at Glendalough. "What do you seek?" asked the saint. "To know Jesus in my heart," replied the young man. With that Kevin invited the youth to step into the lake. He plunged him under the water until the last bubbles of air came from his lips. Then yanking him up by the hair, Kevin asked: "What is it you desire?" "Oh for a breath of fresh air!" gasped the young man. "When you want to know Jesus that much," replied Kevin, "you will surely experience his coming into your heart."

Offer Your Life to God

If we want Jesus to "live in our hearts" (Eph. 3:17) we have to let go of our independence. We do this by *deciding* to offer our lives and our wills to God. This is rather similar to the first three steps of Alcoholics Anonymous. They can be adapted to read:

1. We admitted we were powerless over our restlessness – that in many ways our lives had become meaningless.

2. We came to believe that a Power greater than ourselves could restore our sense of meaning.

3. We made a decision to turn our will and our lives over to God.

Repent by Turning Away From Sin

In the Book of Revelations, Jesus says: "Repent in real earnest, I stand at the door and knock." (3:20).

This means that we have to admit our sins honestly, confess them humbly with a purpose of amendment, and trust confidently in God's mercy. If you are a Catholic, this can be done by availing of the sacrament of reconciliation.

Experience teaches, by the way, that the greatest single obstacle to the spirit of Jesus is an unforgiving heart.

If we harbour resentment against anyone living or dead, we need to forgive them from the heart, trusting in God's grace to do this.

Writing from a Protestant evangelical point of view Billy Graham says: "If you have never accepted Christ into your life, I invite you to do it now before another minute passes. Simply tell God that you know that you are a sinner, and that you are sorry for your sins. Tell Him you believe Jesus Christ died for you, and that you want to give your life to him right now, to follow him as Lord the rest of your life. 'For God so loved the world that he gave his only begotten Son, so that all who believe in him might not perish, but have eternal life'." (Jn 3:16)

Ask Jesus to Come Into Your Heart

We can ask Jesus to come into our hearts with confidence. Scripture says: "This is the confidence which we have in him, that if we ask anything according to his will he hears us. And if we know that he hears us in whatever we ask, we know that we have obtained the requests from him." (1 Jn. 5:14)

Could anything be more in accordance with God's will than that we receive Jesus into our hearts?

The answer is no!

So we say, "Come Lord Jesus" (Rev. 22:20) knowing our prayer *is* being answered.

Submit to God's Grace

Up to this point we have been active – desiring, offering, repenting and asking .

Now it's time to relax. We let go of control.

We trust in God.

He will do the rest.

If the devil tries to discourage us with exaggerated feelings of unworthiness, fear or doubt, we resist him, firm in our faith.

We open the door of our hearts, allowing Jesus to enter our lives by the revelation of his love.

Final Prayer

Lord Jesus, you alone can satisfy the deepest desires of my heart. I offer you my life and my will, knowing you will offer your life to me. Forgive my sins. And now, dear Lord, come into my heart and live within me. I thank you, that even now you are doing this by the outpouring of the Holy Spirit. Amen.

2. BE FILLED WITH THE SPIRIT

Jesus Was Baptised in The Spirit

When Jesus was baptised in the Jordan he not only became the promised Messiah who would be filled with the Spirit of God but shortly afterwards, St. John declared: "He on whom you see the Spirit descend and remain, this is he who is going to *baptise* with the Holy Spirit." (Jn 1:33) This verse sums up the whole purpose of

Jesus' coming, namely, that men and women, in every generation, including our own, would be born again in the Spirit. Before ascending into heaven, Jesus reiterated this point: "While at table with them, he told them not to leave Jerusalem, but to wait for what the Father promised. 'It is,' he said, 'what you have heard me speak about': John baptised with water but, not many days from now, you are going to be *baptised with the Holy Spirit."* (Acts 2:1-5)

These promises were fulfilled in three Pentecosts which show how symbolically the Spirit spread out from the Jews in Jerusalem, to the Gentiles at the end of the earth.

(a) The Pentecost of the Jews (Acts 2:1-5)

(b) The Pentecost of the Samaritans (Acts 8:14-18)

(c) The Pentecost of the Gentiles (Acts 11:1-19)

Baptism in the Spirit
Like Jesus and the first disciples, we modern Christians are called to be filled or to be "baptised in the Spirit" (cf Eph 5:18). The word "baptism" means "to immerse", i.e. to drench, soak, and inundate the personality in the Spirit of God. It is as if the heart, like a sponge, is squeezed until all the darkness of worldliness, selfishness, and pride is forced out and is ready to be saturated in a real, as opposed to a theoretical, knowledge of the love of God. Paul refers to this experience when he writes: "I pray that, according to the riches of his glory, the Father may grant that you may be strengthened in your inner being with power through His Spirit, and that Christ may dwell in your heart through faith, as you are being rooted and grounded in love. I pray that you may have the power to comprehend, with all the saints, what is the breadth and length and height and depth, and to know the love of Christ that surpasses knowledge, so that you may be filled with all the fullness of God." (Eph 3:14-18)

In modern terms, "baptism in the Spirit" is a religious experience that inaugurates anew a decisive awareness of the Presence, power and love of the Lord, active in one's life, which enables the person to live the Christian life in a new way. For example, it is often associated with the reception of one or more of the "charismatic" gifts mentioned by Paul in 1 Cor 12:4-11, such as tongues, mountain-moving faith, healing, prophecy, etc. They are grace-given abilities which equip a person for acts of service which contribute to the renewal and upbuilding of the Church.

What About Baptism and Confirmation?

If Christians receive the Holy Spirit in baptism and confirmation, in what sense, if any, can we say that as adults they are "baptised in the Spirit"? Theologians point out that while we do receive the Holy Spirit in the sacraments of initiation, it is a *theological* rather than an *experiential* event. It is like a child having an inheritance in the bank. The money is there in his name, but it cannot be used until he reaches the age of twenty-one, and signs on the dotted line. Then and only then will he be able to get his hands on the money, to do the things he could only dream of doing beforehand. The same can be true of contemporary Christians. They are heirs to all the blessings that Christ experienced. But until they claim them by faith in the promises of God and through the release of the Holy Spirit within their personalities, they may have the desire, but they will not have the power to do great things for God.

Theologians Mc Donnell and Montague have said that "baptism in the Spirit" is not to be identified with any one group, such as the Charismatic Renewal. Because it belongs to the church as an essential aspect of Christian initiation "it must be taken with ultimate seriousness. Indeed the baptism in the Holy Spirit is normative." (my italics) It is my belief that every bishop, priest and lay person needs to be "baptised in the Spirit" if he or she wants to participate fully in the renewal of the church and in effective evangelization.

How to Be Filled With The Holy Spirit

DARE to ask God for this gift.

Desire to be baptised with the Spirit.
Accept the scriptural promises.
Request God for this gift.
Expect to be blessed by the Spirit.

The Joy of Belonging

1. Desire to be Baptised in the Spirit.

Sometimes the Lord will allow us to experience
(a) considerable suffering e.g. ill health, economic hardship, employment problems, personal unhappiness etc.
(b) temptation and possibly serious sin
(c) the goodness, gifts and holiness of an outstanding Christian in order to reveal our need for God, and to prompt a wholehearted desire for an outpouring of the Holy Spirit, within us.

2. Accept the Scriptural Promises

There is no gift the Lord wants you to receive more than the Holy Spirit. As Jesus said, "I say to you, Ask, and it will be given you; Search and you will find; Knock and the door will be opened for you . . . Is there anyone among you who, if your child asks for a fish, will give a snake instead of a fish? Or if the child asks for an egg, you will give a scorpion? If you then, who are evil, know how to give good gifts to your children, *how much more will the heavenly Father give the Holy Spirit to those who ask him.*" (Lk 11:9-14) In another place he cried out: "Let anyone who is thirsty come to me, and let the one who believes in me drink. As the scripture has said, 'Out of the believer's heart shall flow rivers of living water.' Now he said this about the Spirit, which believers in him were to receive." (Jn 7:37)

3. Request God for This Gift

Say the following prayer or something like it.

"Lord Jesus, I am willing to renounce anything in my life that might grieve your Holy Spirit within me. I want to belong to you from this day forward. I want to be freed from evil, and from all illusions and false inspirations. With your help I will turn away from all wrongdoing and I will avoid anything that might lead me to wrongdoing. I ask you to forgive all the sins that I have committed. I offer my life to you, and I promise to serve you as my Lord. I ask you to baptise me in the Holy Spirit and to give me whatever spiritual gifts you wish me to have. I thank you that my prayer is even now being answered, through Jesus Christ our Lord. Amen."

4. Expect to be Blessed by The Spirit.
If we have prayed in a sincere way, we can expect to be blessed by
God. We may experience the in-filling of the Spirit

(a) in a gradual way by means of almost imperceptible steps of an
incremental kind
(b) in a sudden and dramatic way, associated with feelings of happiness, joy, hope, etc.
(c) in a delayed way. At first nothing seems to happen, and then some
hours, days or even weeks later the person comes into a new experience of God and His love.

Conclusion
People who have been filled with the Spirit, can expect to have a
deeper relationship with God, a greater appetite for prayer, a deeper
insight into scripture and spiritual things in general, a greater love of
people, a new ability to serve others effectively and a renewed desire
to spread the good news about Jesus. Some people will find that they
are granted one or more of the charismatic gifts, e.g. an ability to
pray for the healing of others.

Once we have been filled with the Spirit we will experience a
God-prompted desire to be led like Jesus, by the Spirit (cf Gal 5:25),
and the key to the Christian life is to allow the Spirit to lead. It is a
matter of an inspired ethic and inspired action. When confronted with
any moral decision, great or small, the Christian's first question
should be: "Where does the Holy Spirit lead me in this?"

A recent document makes these pertinent observations: "The
disintegration of family life, the decrease in priestly and religious
vocations, wasteful consumption, forgetfulness of the poor – these
and many other factors are symptoms of the Catholic community's
weakened state. It has left the community prey to the pressures of a
secular world where the media repeatedly mock the Gospel and
cheapen the centrality of a person's worth as a child of God.
Increasingly, many Catholics find it difficult to live according to our
tradition and the teachings of the church." If we are to resist and
reverse this trend we need to be filled with the Spirit. "Fan into a

flame the gift of God that is within you (since receiving baptism and confirmation), for God did not give you a spirit of cowardice, but rather a spirit of power and love and self-discipline." (2 Tim 1:6)

3. THE PROMISES OF GOD

The nature of promises

According to the *Shorter Oxford English Dictionary,* a promise is

(a) a declaration made to another person with respect to the future
(b) stating that one will do, or refrain from, some specified act, or that one will give some specified thing.
So a promise is an undertaking to do, or to give some specified thing. It usually involves some kind of conditions. The promise will be fulfilled, *if* the other party does such and such. We live in a world of broken promises, we can never be sure that people will do what they say they will do. There are a number of reasons why this is so.

• Because the person who undertakes to do something has no intention of doing so.
• It could be that despite his or her best intentions, the one who makes the promise is unable to fulfil it due to lack of the means of doing so.
• Because the second party is unable to satisfy the conditions attached to the promise.

In a religious sense a promise is a divine assurance of future good or blessing. Unlike human promises, God's undertakings can be trusted absolutely because

• He always intends to do what He said He would do. As the Lord says: "By myself I have sworn, from my mouth has gone forth righteousness a word that shall not return." (Is 45:23)
• Unlike human beings, the Lord always has the power to do what he says because "nothing is impossible to God". (Lk 1:37)

Biblical Promises

When people today talk about faith, they are usually referring to a rather static belief in the existence of God. But in the Bible, God's existence is taken for granted. "Only a fool would say in his heart that there is no God," says the psalmist. For their part, when the Jews talked about faith, they were referring to a dynamic belief in the promises of God. In the Old and New Testaments there are many examples of this.

(a) The Lord promised Abraham our "father in faith," that although he and his wife were beyond child-bearing age, they would have a son whose descendants would be as many as the stars in the heavens or the grains of sand on the seashore. In the course of time the promised child was finally born. As St. Paul says, "Yet in view of the promise of God, Abraham didn't waver through unbelief but was strengthened in faith, giving glory to God, being fully aware that *whatever God has promised He will perform* ." (my italics) (Rm 4:20)

(b) Mary is our model of faith in the New Testament. When the angel Gabriel promised that she, a virgin, would become the mother of Jesus by the overshadowing of the Holy Spirit, she responded: "Here am I, the servant of the Lord; let it be with me according to your word." (Lk. 1:38) Sometime later when she visited Elizabeth, her cousin was inspired to declare: "Blessed are you among women . . . *and blessed is she who believed that the promise of God would be fulfilled.*" (my italics) (Lk 1:45) As Heb 11:1 points out: "Faith is the assurance of things hoped for, the conviction of things not seen."

Three Kinds of Scriptural Promises

When you read through the many promises in the books of the Bible it becomes apparent that they can be divided into three groups.

1. Promises of Salvation
In the Old, and especially in the New Testament, the Lord promises to save all those who trust in him by forgiving their sins and by

pouring out his Holy Spirit of love upon them. For example in Ezch 36:25-28 we read this famous promise which came to fulfilment on the day of Pentecost: "I will sprinkle clean water upon you, and you shall be clean from all your uncleannesses, and from all your idols I will cleanse you. A new heart I will give you, a new spirit I will put within you; and I will remove from your body the heart of stone and give you a heart of flesh. I will put my Spirit within you, and make you follow my statutes and be careful to observe my ordinances." In the New Testament St. Paul promises us that "If you confess with your mouth Jesus as Lord, and believe in your heart that God raised Him from the dead, you shall be saved." (Rm 10:9).

2. Promises of Help for Living The Christian Life

Arguably there are three kinds of promise under this heading:

(a) Promises that God will give us the strength to live the Christian life as Jer 17:7 assures us: "The Lord blesses those who put their trust in him." This is what Paul discovered. He declared, "God's grace is sufficient for us, for his power is made perfect in weakness . . . *I can do everything* (my italics) through him who gives me strength." (2 Cor 12:9; Phil 4:13)

(b) Faith that in His providence God will provide as he does for the birds of the air and the lilies in the field. As Jesus promised: "Strive first for the kingdom of God and his righteousness, and all else will be added to you." (Mt 6:33)

(c) The assurance that God will enable us to overcome evil of all kinds. As Jesus promised: "In the world you will have many troubles, I have overcome the world." (Jn 16:33) And St Paul says: "God is faithful, and He will not let you be tested beyond your strength, but with the testing He will provide the way out so that you may be able to endure it." (1 Cor 10:13)

3. Promises of Resurrection and Eternal Life
All of us have to die, but the scriptures assure us that all those who are united to Christ will be raised to glory on the last day. For example, Jesus promised, "Those who eat my flesh and drink my

blood have eternal life, and I will raise them up on the last day." (Jn 6:54)

Claiming the Pomises

(a) If we want to have faith in the promises of God we must first have faith in the God of the promises. For more on this see the two previous chapters. As St. Paul reminds us: "He who has promised is faithful," (Heb 10:23) and "If we are faithless, he remains faithful – for he cannnot deny himself." (2 Tim 2 :13)

(b) When reading the scriptures, notice the many promises they contain. They provide for every conceivable need. Some people like to underline them with a distinctive colour.

(c) Arguably the promises to do with petitionary prayer are not only the most challenging but also the most important. Consider the following examples.
• "Truly, truly, I say to you, the one who believes in me, will also do the works that I do and, in fact, will do greater works than these, because I am going to the Father. I will do whatever you ask in my name, so that the Father may be glorified in the Son. If in my name you ask me for anything, I will do it." (Jn 14:12-15)
• "Ask, and it shall be given to you . . . for the one who asks receives." (Mt. 7:7)
• "Therefore I say you, all things for which you pray and ask believe that you have received them, and they shall be granted to you." (Mt 21:22)
• "And in that day you will ask me no question. Truly, truly, I say to you, if you shall ask the Father for anything, he will give it to you in my name. Until now you have asked for nothing in my name; ask and you will receive, that your joy may be full." (Jn 16:23)

(d) Like Mary before us, we need to ponder words like these in our hearts. As Prov 4:20-21 advises us: "My child, be attentive to my words; incline your ear to my sayings. Do not let them escape from your sight, keep them within your heart." We can do this by reading and praying the scriptures in the way outlined later in this section.

(e) We need to remember that we have conditions to fulfil before we can claim the promises. For example 2 Chron 7:14 contains four conditions and three interrelated promises: "*If* my people who bear my name humble themselves, and pray and seek my presence and turn from their wicked way, *then* I will listen from heaven and forgive their sins and restore their country." So if you wish to claim any promise, ask yourself the question, "What does God expect of me?"

Although many a harassed person has turned to our Lord's reassuring words: "Come to me, all that are weary and are carrying heavy burdens, and I will give you rest," many of them fail to go on to the next verse where the conditions are mentioned: "*Take* my yoke upon you, (i.e. the great commandment of love) and *learn* from me; for I am *gentle* and *humble* of heart, and you will find rest for your souls. For my yoke is easy and my burden is light." (Mt 11:28-30)

There are a number of conditions to be satisfied before God will carry out His promise to answer prayers of petition e.g. they need to be made in the name of Jesus, without resentment, in communion with others, in accord with the Lord's will, with thanksgiving, perseverance and expectant faith. See more on petitionary prayer, later in this section.

Conclusion
If we are going to "walk by faith and not by sight," as Paul instructs us in 2 Cor 5:7, we will have to rely in all things upon the mighty promises of Christ. To do this we need to ask Mary to intercede on our behalf: "Pray for us, O most holy mother of God, that we may be worthy of the promises of Christ."

4. PRAYER AS FRIENDSHIP WITH GOD

Classic Descriptions of Prayer
St Gregory of Nyssa wrote: "Prayer is a conference or conversation of the soul with God."

St Francis de Sales wrote: "Prayer is conversation, a discussion, or dialogue of the soul with God. By prayer we speak to God and God in turn speaks to us. We aspire to Him and breathe in Him; He likewise inspires us and breathes upon us."

St Teresa of Avila wrote: "Prayer is nothing other than an intimate friendship, a frequent heart-to-heart conversation, with Him by Whom we know ourselves to be loved."

There are two aspects to the prayerful kind of dialogue referred to by the saints:

1. Honest self-disclosure of thoughts, feelings and desires to God.
2. Loving attention to God's revelation of himself.

Prayer as Self-disclosure

St. Aelred of Rievaulx wrote: "A friend shares all the innermost secrets of your heart . . . to him you confide everything as if he were your other self."

Because we know that Jesus loves us as our dearest friend, we disclose all our innermost secrets to him. Why share such things with the Lord? Doesn't he know them anyway? True, but he wants us to reveal our real selves to him, not because he needs it, but because he knows we do. There are three reasons for this.

1. The impulse of love is to give. The greatest gift we can give the Lord is the gift of our true selves.

2. We will never feel that we are truly loved and accepted by the Lord until we know he loves and accepts us as we are.

3. This kind of honesty opens the heart to revelation. The extent that we hide our experiences from Jesus is the extent to which we will be closed to his inspirations.

What Should We Disclose in Prayer?

Personal prayer goes beyond facts and ideas, to share deeper feelings. We tell Jesus about our reactions

1. to God Himself, such as fear of His demands, gratitude for His gifts, anger for taking a loved one, etc.

2. to everyday events, such as a family worry, joyful news, a hurtful remark, upsetting reports on T.V. about wars, famines and acts of violence, etc.

3. to ourselves such as guilt, anger because of failure, or satisfaction in creating something or doing some task well, etc.

Usually, it's not difficult to share positive feelings with Jesus. The trouble arises when we try to come before Him, not in our Sunday best, but in the ragged clothes of our anger, fear and guilt. There seems to be three ways in which we can cope with negative feelings like these.

1. Excessive self-reference by being honest with oneself in the presence of God about what one feels, rather than being honest *to the God* who is present.

2. Repression of feelings such as anger with God, as wrong. When they are buried alive they turn into numbing states of anxiety and depression. Prayer becomes formal. We go through the motions but not surprisingly the Lord seems distant and unreal.

*3. Expres*sion of negative feelings without censorship or editing to the Lord.

Prayer as Loving Attention to God
The Lord wants to reveal his presence to all of us. As we desire to know him better, we ask to "see him more clearly . . . day by day." He responds by revealing himself in the following ways:

1. Through Scripture: The biblical books, especially the gospels, are a privileged place of divine revelation. So in the words of one hymn we pray: "In the scriptures by the Spirit may we see the Saviour's face." As we meet with Jesus in the gospels, we often find that our hearts "Burn within us" (Lk. 24:32) as we begin to have an inner sense of who he is as God's Son. For more on this see "Reading and Praying the Scriptures" above.

2. Through People: Sometimes as we listen to other people, especially when they are sharing their experience of God with us, we can find ourselves responding with peace, joy, awe, love, etc. These feelings are evoked by the awareness of a mysterious Presence, greater than the person we are talking to. As the poet Hopkins wrote: "Christ plays in ten thousand places, lovely in limbs and lovely in eyes not his, to the Father through the features of men's faces."

3. Through nature: Creation is the Lord's work of art. As we come to appreciate its beauty, we can also come to experience the Presence of its Creator. St Paul reminds us: "Ever since the creation of the world, God's eternal power and divine nature, invisible though they are, have been understood and seen through the things he has made." (Rm 1:20) As one hymn puts it: "The Father gave his children the wonder of the world, in which his power and glory like banners are unfurled."

4. Through Art: Music, painting, poetry, etc., can mediate something of the Presence of the Lord. For example, Milton described how church music affected him in these words: "Let the pealing organ blow . . . As may with sweetness, through mine ear, dissolve me into ecstasies and bring all heaven before mine eyes."

Prayer a Search for God's Will
The Lord also wants to reveal his *will* to us. As St. Vincent de Paul wrote: "Prayer is a conversation of the soul with God, a mutual communication in which God interiorly tells the soul what He wishes it to do and in which the soul tells its God what He Himself has taught it to ask for." He does this in a number of ways.

1. When we become aware of Who God is and what He is like, He seems to say to our hearts: "Be for others what I am for you" e.g. if in prayer you found me to be compassionate, accepting, forgiving,

understanding etc. then be compassionate, accepting, forgiving and understanding in your dealings with others.

2. A line of scripture may have been dead on the page as far as we were concerned. Suddenly, by God's grace it jumps alive into the heart as an inspired word of guidance e.g. by telling us not to be afraid, to reverence the poor as if they were Christ himself, to love enemies etc.

3. The Holy Spirit can prompt all kinds of holy desires and inspirations in our hearts. They can come in the form of thoughts, images, feelings, longings and the like. We will know that they are from God if they lead to a deeper relationship with the Lord and are associated with inner peace and joy.When the Lord reveals his Presence and his Word to us we are empowered to live as the children of God and the friends of Jesus.

5. READING AND PRAYING THE SCRIPTURES

All Scripture Focuses on Christ

(a) *The Old Testament Points to Christ*

All the books of the Old Testament, point to Christ and find their fulfilment in him. Jesus himself made this clear to the two disciples on the road to Emmaus. They poured out their sorrows to this stranger whom they surprisingly failed to recognize. "Jesus replied: 'You foolish men! so slow to believe the full message of the prophets! Was it not ordained that the Christ should suffer and so enter into his glory?' Then starting with Moses and going through all the prophets he explained to them the passages throughout the Scriptures that were about himself." (Lk. 24:25-28)

(b)*The New Testament Reveals Christ*

The words and actions of Jesus are recorded in the Gospels. They are like so many panes of glass in the window of his humanity. When they are illuminated by the light of the Holy Spirit and viewed with the eyes of faith, they can become a unique source of revelation.

Through them we begin to see what God is like. As Jesus said: "To have seen me is to have seen the Father." (Jn. 14:9). The remaining books of the New Testament record the impact and implications of Christ for the first Christians.

Why Read the Scriptures in a Prayerful Way?

1. St. Jerome provides the first and most powerful motive: "The person who doesn't know the scriptures doesn't know Jesus Christ!"

2. The Bible is unlike any other book because "All scripture is inspired by God . . . The Word of God is something alive and active . . . It can judge the secret thoughts and emotions of the heart." (2 Tim. 3:1; Heb. 4:12)

3. St. Paul says that scripture "is useful for teaching the truth, rebuking error, correcting faults, and giving instruction for living." (2 Tim. 3:1)

4. St. Paul says that the word of God is the "sword of the Spirit". (Eph. 6:17) It can be used in times of temptation to ward off the influence of the evil one. This is what Jesus did when he was tempted by Satan in the wilderness.

5. To ponder the scriptures in a prayerful way increases faith. St. Paul wrote: "Faith comes by hearing the living word of God." (Rm. 10:17)

Reading and Sharing the Scriptures With Others
The following method is known as *paired sharing*. It can be used by two people, a family, or a larger group.

1. You could begin with either of the following prayers, both of which are to be found in the Divine Office:

(a) "In the scriptures by the Spirit,
     May we see the Saviour's face,
     Hear his word and heed his calling,
     Know his will and grow in grace".

(b) "Bright as fire in darkness,
Sharper than a sword,
Lives through the ages,
God's eternal word.
May that word dwell richly in our hearts through faith, and so
bear the fruit of good works in the future."

2. One person reads a chosen passage slowly, out loud e.g. the Gospel for the following Sunday, or one chosen from the Bible. The other person(s) listen without reading the text.

3. During one minute's silence, each person tries to recall as much of the passage as possible.

4. One person re-reads the passage out loud. This time each person follows the text in his or her Bible or missal.

5. Each person says a private prayer to the Holy Spirit asking for understanding and inspiration. They then spend three minutes mulling over the passage, pausing at any word, phrase, idea or image which is striking .

6. Share what you have received as a result of your prayerful reflection with one other person. If it is not too embarrassing, try to look your partner in the eye as you share.

7. If it seems appropriate, individuals can share their insights and personal responses with the larger group.

8. The session ends with a prayer of gratitude. Thank God for helping the word to leap off the printed page in such a way that it makes the heart burn within. (c.f. Lk. 24:32)

How to Pray the Scriptures in Private
In this section we will look at the famous Benedictine method of scriptural prayer. It evolves through the four stages of reading, meditating, praying and contemplating biblical texts. A 12th century monk described its purpose in these words: "Reading, you should seek; meditating, you will find; praying, you shall call; and contemplating, the door will be opened to you."

1. Kiss the Bible as a sign of reverence for God's word.

2. Say the prayer for guidance in point 1 of the previous section.

3. Choose the passage that you intend to read e.g. the gospel for the following Sunday, or one that relates to your personal needs.

4. *Read* the passage slowly two or three times. St. Anselm wrote: "The scriptures are not to be read in a noisy situation, but where things are quiet, not superficially and in a rush, but a little at a time." It's a good idea to read the passage out loud in a whisper at least, until a phrase, an image, a sentence or a word catches your attention in a special way.

5. *Meditate* on the meaning of these outstanding verses. As the Lord says: "Pay attention to my words, listen carefully to my utterances. I say, do not let them out of your sight, keep them deep in your heart. They are life to those who grasp them, health for the entire body." (Prov. 4:20-23)

There are two ways of carrying out this advice:

(a) If you are reflecting on a doctrinal point e.g. from the letters of St. Paul, it can be helpful if you repeat a chosen word or sentence over and over again, while letting its meaning sink into the heart. It's rather like sucking a lozenge. You let it dissolve in order to savour its taste and flavour.

(b) If you are reflecting on a scriptural story or parable e.g. one from the gospels it can be helpful to imagine the incident as if it were a video. *See* the scene and the characters who are involved; you may choose to be one of them, e.g. an onlooker in the crowd when Jesus is healing a blind man. *Hear* what is said. You may want to augment dialogue in the text with some of your own. *Notice* what the characters do. *Sense* what they feel, and try to be aware of you own personal emotional reaction to the text.

6. *Pray* from the heart, allowing rational reflection to become conversation with the Lord. St. Vincent de Paul wrote: "The soul is like a sailboat equipped with oars. The oars are not used unless the

wind fails, and then progress isn't as rapid or pleasant as when the ship is moving along under a fair breeze. Similarly, we have need of reflection in prayer when special assistance from the Holy Spirit is not forthcoming, but when the heavenly breeze blows upon the heart, we must yield ourselves to its influence." We do this when we tell the Lord about our feelings of love, joy, gratitude, sorrow, repentance, desire, enthusiasm, conviction and commitment, evoked by reflection on the text. In this regard St. Benedict said: "Let the prayer be brief and pure." Once distractions occur go back to reading and reflecting in the way described, until you can pray again.

7. *Contemplate* by being still and resting in the Lord. Reflection and prayerful conversation with the Lord can give way to a sense of union with Christ. St. Vincent de Paul says: "It is not the result of human teaching. It is not attainable by human effort, and it is not bestowed on everyone . . . In this state of quiet, the soul finds itself suddenly filled with spiritual illuminations and holy affections."

8. *Action:* As a result of prayer we begin to see Jesus more clearly and to love him more dearly. This leads to a desire to follow him more nearly in everyday life. It's good to make a resolution that flows from the scripture text e.g. to be more forgiving. St. Vincent de Paul says that such resolutions should be Single, Precise, Definite and Possible. As Jesus observed: "The seeds that fell in good soil stand for those who hear the message and retain it in a good and obedient heart, and they persist until they bear fruit." (Lk. 8:15)

6. THE POWER OF PETITIONARY PRAYER

Disappointment in Prayer

Most people ask God for graces and favours. Some do so with great intensity and sincerity. Yet despite Christ's promises to answer prayer, they often experience disappointment. The ailing child eventually dies. The unemployed relative fails to get a job. The woman enduring arthritic pain continues to suffer. Not surprisingly the question is asked: "Why doesn't God respond to my requests?"

Ultimately only the Lord knows, as scripture says: "Who has known the mind of the Lord?" (Rm. 11:34) That said, Jesus does teach in the Gospels that our petitions will be answered when certain dispositions are present. We will look at seven of these because they are often overlooked by those who pray.

Becoming Worthy of The Promises of Christ

1. Praying in the Name of Jesus

Jesus once said (Jn. 16:23): "I tell you most solemnly, anything you ask for from the Father, He will grant in my *name*. Until now you have not asked for anything in my *name*. Ask and you will receive, and so your joy will be completed."

We can only pray in the name of Jesus, when we have a deep personal relationship with him, as our closest and dearest friend.When this is so we have a personal conviction that:

(a) All of our sins are completely forgiven and forgotten. As St. Paul wrote: "There is now no condemnation awaiting those who belong to Christ Jesus." (Rm. 8:1)

(b) Just as the Father loved Jesus, so he loves us. The Holy Spirit gives us the power, in the words of Paul, "to understand how broad and long, how high and deep, is Christ's love . . . and so be completely filled with the very nature of God." (Eph. 3:18)

(c) If God loves us so much he would want to bless us. Jesus referred to this when he said: "If you who are evil know how to give good gifts to your children, how much more will the Father in heaven give good things to those who ask Him!" (Mt.7:11) St. Paul echoes this when he says: "If God has given us His Son would He not give us all things in Him." (Rm. 8:32)

So when we pray: "Heavenly Father, I ask you in the name of Jesus to do such and such", we are praying in the awareness of the boundless mercy, love and generosity of the God who says to us: "All I have is yours." (Lk. 15:31)

2. Praying Without Resentment

In Mk. 11:21-25, Jesus says that prayer will be answered, even to the point of miracles, but then he adds: "And when you stand and pray, forgive whatever you have against anybody, so that your Father in Heaven may forgive your failings too." (Mk. 11:25)

While God's mercy is always available to us, we only experience it inwardly when we are willing to forgive those who trespass against us. All of us suffered hurts at home, at school and in adult life. We consciously remember some of these hurts; others which were never resolved have sunk with their negative feelings and attitudes into the realm of the unconscious. One way or another, they tend to eclipse the heart's ability to savour inwardly the mercy, love and generosity of God. So it is necessary to ask the Holy Spirit to recall if there is any person from the past who stands in need of your forgiveness. Then one has to make the *decision* to forgive with the aid of God's grace c.f. "Forgiveness and Healing", in *Growing in Health and Grace,* (Campus Publishing, Galway, 1991). Remember what Jesus said: "Whatever measure you use to give – large or small – will be used to measure what is given back to you." (Lk. 6:38)

3. Praying With Unity of Mind and Heart
Jesus tells us that prayers of petition are powerful when they are offered by members of the community who are one in mind and heart. "Again, I tell you, if two of you agree on earth about anything you ask, it will be done for you by my Father in heaven. For where two or three are gathered in my name, I am there among them." (Mt 18:19-20) Over the years I have discovered that it is the Holy Spirit that brings about the agreement referred to by Jesus by independently prompting different people to pray for the same thing e.g. that the ailing son of a mutual friend might recover from his illness.

4. Pray in Accord With God's Will
In The Lord's Prayer Jesus taught us to say: "Thy will be done on earth as it is in heaven." Clearly, therefore, we should ask God for graces and favours that are in agreement with His will. In his letter St. James writes: "Why you don't have what you want is because you don't pray for it. When you pray, you don't get it. It is because you have prayed for something to indulge your own desires." (4:3) Sometimes what we want is downright *sinful* e.g. praying that an

adulterous relationship would not be discovered. More often than not our prayers are *misguided*. The general aim is O.K. e.g. that a husband or child stop drinking, but the means are wrong. We ask the Lord to change the other person, when it might be wiser to ask the Lord to change us by helping us to accept and love the drinker unconditionally. The Lord could then use that kind of attitude to give the drinker both the *desire* and the *power* to change. In the words of St. Paul we should pray "that through perfect wisdom and spiritual understanding we will reach the fullest knowledge of God's will." (Col. 1:9) St. James says that if we pray without a shadow of a doubt, such wisdom will be given. (cf. Jm. 1:2-8)

5. Pray With Thanksgiving

On a number of occasions the New Testament tells us to pray with thanksgiving.
• "Pray constantly, and for *all things* give thanks to God".
• *"Always* give thanks for *everything* to God the Father".
• "If there is anything you need, pray for it, asking God for it with prayer and *thanksgiving."* (1 Thess. 5:18, Eph. 5:19, Phil. 4:6-7)
No matter what our need or suffering, we should pray with thanksgiving, in the belief that God will bring good out of the negative circumstances of our lives, and that a treasure of blessing lies hidden in the field of our adversity. St. Paul wrote: "We know that by turning *everything* to their good, God cooperates with those who love Him." (Rm. 8:28) Many of us have found that as we raised our hearts to God in prayer with thanksgiving, we were opening ourselves to receive the grace He wanted to give us.

6. Pray With Perseverance

On a number of occasions Jesus told the disciples – and us – to pray without ceasing .
• "Ask and it will be given you . . . for the one who asks always receives." (Mt.7:7) In the Greek of the New Testament the word "ask" is in the continuous present i.e. "keep on asking".
• At the end of the parable of the importunate friend Jesus says: "I tell you, if the man does not get up and give the bread to him for friendship sake, persistence will be enough to make him get up and give his friend all he wants." (Lk. 11:9-13)

• At the end of the parable of the unjust judge, Jesus says: "Now will not God see justice done to his chosen who cry to him day and night even if he delays to help them?" (Lk. 18:1-8) Why does God delay? Perhaps it is to purify and deepen our desire. He may be schooling us in patience and trust. He may be waiting for the right moment, the moment of saving grace.

7. Pray With Expectant Faith

Many people believe the promises of Christ with their *minds*. But in everyday situations we find them hard to trust with our *hearts*. Mental faith prays in the hope that God may do something in the future. Heartfelt faith prays with the *conviction* that God *is* doing something in the *present*. When the woman with the severe bleeding reached out for healing, she didn't say: "If I touch the hem of his garment I may be healed", rather she asserted: "I will be healed." (Mk. 5:28) This illustrates the kind of faith Jesus spoke of when he said: *"Whatever you ask in prayer, believing you have it already,* it will be yours." (Mk. 11:24) Remember, Jesus never said to anyone: "Your hope has made you well."

7. THE PRAYER OF PRAISE

The Importance of Praise

There are two main forms of prayer – petition and worship.

1. By means of *petitionary prayer* we ask God for the graces and blessings we need.We do this in a spirit of expectant faith knowing that Jesus promised "ask and you shall receive". (Lk. 11:19) But when the Father grants our requests, need should give way to gratitude, petition to praise. Otherwise there is a danger that we would end up trying to focus God's attention on us, rather than focusing our attention on Him.

2. The word *worship* comes from Anglo-Saxon. It means to know "the worth" of someone. We worship God when we begin to appreciate His wonderful Power and Presence. Religious worship is

like a bridge that enables us to cross over from worldly concerns into the awareness of God. Praise is a keystone in this bridge, flanked on either side by thanksgiving and adoration.

(a) Worship as *thanksgiving* begins in the grateful awareness of *the gifts* of God.

(b) Worship as *praise* is deepened when we come to appreciate *the giver* of the gifts.

(c) Worship as *adoration* comes to maturity as we begin to respond to the revelation of *God's glory*.

Motives For Praising God

1. We were created to praise God

What brings human fulfilment? Pleasure, said Freud. Power, said Adler. Meaning, said Frankl. But surely St. Augustine was correct when he said that *our hearts are restless until they rest in God*. The prayer of praise is our response to the experience of the Lord. It is our deepest vocation and destiny. That is why the Shorter Westminster Catechism says: "Men's chief end is to glorify God, and to enjoy him forever." This echoes the inspired words of St. Paul: "We who have first hoped in Christ, have been destined and appointed to live for the praise of his glory." (Eph. 1:12)

2. Scripture Urges Us to Praise God

All through the Bible we are urged to praise God. For example in Rev. 19:5-7 we read: "There came from the throne (of God) the sound of a voice saying: 'Praise our God, all his servants and all people, both great and small, who worship him!' Then I heard what sounded like the sound of a roaring waterfall, like loud peals of thunder. I heard them say, 'Praise God! For the Lord, our Almighty God, is King! Let us rejoice and be glad; let us praise his greatness'." Surely the only reasonable response to such a heavenly invitation is to join Mary in saying: "My soul magnifies the Lord, and my spirit rejoices in God my Saviour." (Lk. 1:46-47)

3. *Praise Helps Us to Grow in Holiness.*

The prayer of praise helps us to escape the gravitational pull of self-absorption and to become absorbed in awareness of God. Like gaily coloured kites, our minds are borne aloft in praise, not that God needs our praises. Our desire to praise Him is itself His gift. Our praise adds nothing to His greatness, but it helps us to grow in his grace. As Ps. 22:3 puts it: "God lives in the praises of His people." As we open our hearts in praise, they become like chalices into which the wine of God's Spirit is poured. He fills us with a sense of His Presence until our hearts brim over with joy. This in turn prompts us to praise Him all the more. And so it goes on. Praise then, is our short-cut to holiness.

4. *Praise Delivers Us From All Evil*

We all experience temptation. But St. Paul assures us that "The shield of faith will put *out all the fiery darts* of the Evil One." (Eph. 6:16) In a number of places in the Old Testament we are told that the *Lord is our shield.* Instead of wrestling in vain with evil, we nestle in the Lord by faith. We express that faith by praising Him, Whose Name is above all names. As we concentrate on glorifying Him, He concentrates on shielding us from every evil.

5. *Praise Anticipates the Help of God in Adversity.*

Our God is not a God of defeat but a God of victory. During times of adversity we acknowledge this in our praises. Instead of magnifying our problems by focusing on them with anxiety, we magnify the Lord by focusing on Him with confidence. We have every reason for doing this. The Lord has said: "Do not be afraid or disturbed, *the battle is mine, not yours.*" As we praise God in adversity we anticipate the help he is going to give us. Like the people at Jericho, we discover that faith expressed in praise can overcome impossible odds, because "with God nothing is impossible." (Lk. 1:37)

6. *Praise is a Preparation For Heaven*

In Rev. 19:6, the life of heaven is described in these words: "I heard what seemed to be the loud voice of a great multitude in heaven crying, Alleluia, salvation, and glory, and power belong to God." Aware of God's glory, the angels and saints send one thunderous wave of praise after another, up to the throne of God. When we praise the Lord.

• We *echo* in our hearts something of the heavenly worship.

• We begin to serve on earth an *apprenticeship* for what we will do eternally in paradise.

• We express our *hope* in the resurrection and in our final salvation.

Some Means of Praising God

1. Make a Commitment to Praise God

Once we appreciate the importance of glorifying the Lord, we should make an unconditional *decision* to praise him every day. So when we have negative feelings during times of adversity we express them honestly to the Lord. But then we go on to express our faith convictions in praise. As one hymn puts it: "I have decided to praise the Lord, no matter how I feel. God is always real. I have decided to praise the Lord. I'll praise him when I'm happy; I'll praise him when I'm sad; I'll praise Him when I'm good; I'll praise Him when I'm bad; I'll praise Him when I'm up; I'll praise Him when I'm down; I'll praise Him when I'm weary; I'll praise Him when I'm strong. I have decided to praise the Lord."

2. Food For Praise

(a) As we read the scriptures we begin to see the Lord more clearly. As we learn to appreciate Him in this way we grow in the desire to praise Him. Not only that, the psalms in particular show us *how* to praise God.

(b) As we spend time in personal prayer, we enter into a deeper conscious awareness of the Lord and His gifts. As we learn to know and love Him, we express our admiration in praise.Without this kind of personal prayer, we might honour the Lord with our lips, but our hearts would be far from Him.

(c) Everything is beautiful. As we become sensitive to the wonders of nature, we will want to praise the Divine Artist, for creation, and on its behalf. In this way we become ambassadors of praise, representing the dandelion in the field, and the pike and trout hiding in deep pools.

3. Praise With Enthusiasm

An Irish verse says: "Only a fool would fail to praise God in His might, when the tiny mindless birds, praise Him in their flight." Sir.43:30 goes even further: "When you praise the Lord, exalt Him as much as you can; for He will surpass even that. When you exalt Him, put forth all your strength, and do not grow weary, for you cannot praise Him enough."

8. DISCERNING THE PRESENCE AND POWER OF GOD

God's Presence in Our Lives

The second question in Herbert McCabe's *New Catechism* asks: "What does God want for His creatures?" and answers: "God wants each kind of creature to flourish in the way appropriate to it, and He wants His human creatures not only to flourish in a human way but to share His own life and happiness for ever." The Lord satisfies His desire for communion with us in two main ways.

1. The Lord Prompts Holy Desires in The Heart.

God draws us to Himself. He does this by means of the holy desires, longings and yearning He prompts within us. They seek relationship with Him, through Jesus His Son. As the Lord said in Jn. 6:44: "No one can come to Me, unless the Father who sent Me draws him to Me." St. Paul witnessed to this inward drawing of the Father when he wrote in Phil. 3:10: "All I want is to know Christ and to experience the power of his resurrection ." These moving words find an echo in the well-known prayer of St. Richard of Chichester (d. 1283): "Day by day, O Lord, three things I pray: To see thee more clearly, to love thee more dearly, and to follow thee more nearly, day by day."

2. The Lord Satisfies Our Desires by Revealing Himself to Us

Having planted holy desires in our hearts, it is not surprising to find that repeatedly the Lord promises to satisfy them.
• Jer. 33:3: "Call to me and I will answer you, and will tell you great and hidden things that you have not known."

• In Is 48:6-7 we read, "From this time forward I make you hear new things, hidden things that you have not known. They are created now, not long ago; before today you have never heard of them, so that you could not say, 'I already knew them'."

• In Jer. 31:31-34 we read how this wonderful revelation will take place: "I will put my laws into their minds, and I will write them upon their hearts . . . None of them will have to teach his fellow countryman to know the Lord, because all will know Me, from the least to the greatest."

These promises find their fulfilment with the outpouring of the Holy Spirit. As Jesus said in Jn. 16:13, "The Spirit reveals the truth about God." St. Paul puts it this way in 1 Cor. 2:9-16: "What no eye has seen nor ear heard . . . God revealed to us through the Spirit. For the Spirit searches everything, even the depths of God . . . Now we have received not the Spirit of the world, but the Spirit which is from God . . . We have the mind of Christ."

The Purpose of a Discernment Method
In the light of the above points, the purpose of a discernment method is threefold.

(a) It helps to focus attention on God-given desires, and to notice the things that may be blocking them.

(b) It enables a person to become aware of the presence and inspirations of the Lord. It also looks at a person's *reactions* and *responses* to such revelations.

(c) In the words of 1 Jn. 4: 1, it develops the ability to "test the spirits to see whether they are of God." St. Ignatius of Loyola wrote in par. 32 of his *Spiritual Exercises:* "There are three kinds of thought in the mind, namely: one which is strictly my own, and arises wholly from my own free will; two others which come from without, the one from the good Spirit, the other from the Evil One."

A Discernment Exercise
1. Relax your body.
2. Calm your mind and imagination.

3. Affirm in faith that God is present.

4. Consider these words of Cardinal Newman: "God's presence is not discerned at the time it is upon us, but afterwards when we look back upon what is gone and over."

5. Ask the Holy Spirit to guide your discernment exercise: "Lord, you enlighten every heart. Enlighten mine to recognize how you have been drawing me to yourself. Help me to appreciate your Presence and to distinguish those inspirations that came from You, and those that came from either myself or from the Evil One."

6. During the recent past, when were you most aware of the Lord's presence? Was it at Mass, when praying, reading the scriptures, enjoying nature, talking with a friend, etc?

7. What did you experience when the Lord revealed Himself to you? Was it joy, awe, peace, fear, hope, encouragement, etc? Did you tell the Lord what you felt?

8. What did you notice about the Person of the Lord when he revealed Himself to you that would account for the feelings evoked within you? Was He compassionate, accepting, attentive, understanding, loving, angry, etc?

9. How did you decide to respond to the revelation of the Lord? Did it find expression in a prayerful way, e.g. in gratitude and praise? Did it find expression in any kind of resolution, e.g. to be reconciled to someone, to avoid temptation, etc?

10. Were you aware of any promptings or inspirations of the the recent past? Did you respond to them or not?

11. Did you experience any kind of negative inspiration, feeling, attitude, mood, desire which may have led to a negative and sinful thought, word or deed in the recent past? If so, tell the Lord that you are sorry for having saddened the Holy Spirit, and ask for His forgiveness with confidence.

12.Thank God for the graces He has given you in the recent past and ask His blessing upon your future.

Some Concluding Observations

1. How Often Should The Discernment Method Be Used?

As often as you like. But most people find that once a week is enough. Anything more could be impractical.

2. How Much Time Should Be Spent on The Exercise?

Normally, between five and fifteen minutes will be sufficient. During a retreat one might spend a bit longer.

3. Should The Results of The Discernment Be Written Down?

Strictly speaking, it isn't necessary to write down the results of the discernment exercise. However, to do so can have distinct advantages.

(a) To express something on paper has the effect of impressing it upon the mind and memory.

(b) To review one's notes after a few months could reveal interesting and important trends, that might otherwise be overlooked

(c) If one is fortunate to have a spiritual director, notes of the discernment exercise can be very useful as a basis for conversation.

(d) During times of darkness and desolation, the recorded account of past graces and consolations can be a source of encouragement.

(e) The written highlights of the discernment process can be used as the starting points for future periods of prayer.

9. DEVOTION TO THE HOLY SPIRIT

When I was a student I came across these words of Cardinal Mercier (1851-1926) who was archbishop of Malines and primate of Belgium. They have inspired me ever since.

"I am going to reveal to you the secret of sanctity and happiness. For five minutes every day control your imagination and close your eyes to the things of sense and your ears to all the noises of the world, in order to enter into yourself. Then, in

the sanctity of your baptized soul which is the temple of the
Holy Spirit speak to that Divine Spirit, saying to Him;

O, Holy Spirit, beloved of my soul, I adore You. Enlighten me,
guide me, strengthen me, console me. Tell me what I should do.
Give me Your orders. I promise to submit myself to all that You
desire of me and to accept all that You permit to happen to me.
Let me only know Your will.

If you do this, your life will flow along happily, serenely and
full of consolation, even in the midst of trials. Grace will be
proportioned to the trial, giving you the strength to carry it and
you will arrive at the gate of Paradise, laden with merit. This
submission to the Holy Spirit is the secret of sanctity."

A few years ago, inspired by Cardinal Mercier's example, I felt that
the Lord was leading me to write a contemporary prayer to the Holy
Spirit, one that could be said every morning and evening.

Daily Prayer to the Holy Spirit

May He strengthen you inwardly through the working of His Spirit.
(Eph. 3:16)

To Be Said in The Morning

Relax your body . . .

Calm your mind and imagination . . .

Affirm that God is present . . .

Ponder these words from scripture . . .

Be filled with the Spirit, Be guided by the Spirit, Walk by the Spirit.
(Eph. 5:18; Gal. 5:16 & 5:25)

Prayer For The Divine Indwelling.
Father in heaven,
Yours is a Spirit of truth and love.
• Pour that same Holy Spirit into my body, mind and soul.
• Preserve me this day from all illusions and false inspirations and
• Reveal Your presence and Your word to me in a way I can
understand.

94

I thank You that You will do this, while giving me the ability to respond, through Jesus Christ our Lord. Amen.
(Pause for a moment's reflection)

To be said at night

Relax your body . . .

Calm your mind and imagination . . .

Affirm that God is present . . .

Prayers For Discernment

Father in heaven,

Help me to recall with gratitude those occasions when I was aware of Your presence today and to savour again what You meant to me . . .
(Pause for a moment's reflection)

Help me to become aware of the promptings and inspirations you have given me today and to know whether I responded to them or not . . .
(Pause for a moment's reflection)

Enlighten my heart to recognise any unloving feeling, mood, attitude, desire, thought, word or deed that saddened your Holy Spirit today . . .
(Pause for a moment's reflection)

Final Prayer
Father in heaven,
Thank you for the gift of Your Spirit.
Today it has urged me
to see You more clearly,
to love You more dearly.
and to follow You more nearly.
As for my shortcomings, please forgive them.
And now, bless me as I sleep, so that refreshed by Your Spirit, I may rise to praise You, through Jesus Christ our Lord.
Amen.

About This Daily Prayer

Recent popes have said that the Holy Spirit is the key to personal and Church renewal.

In 1961, on the eve of the Second Vatican Council, Pope John XXIII prayed to the Lord in these words: "Renew your wonders in this our day as by a new Pentecost." (*Humanae Salutis*)

Fourteen years later in 1975, Pope Paul VI could write: "We see the Church today in an age dominated as it were, by the Holy Spirit. The faithful are striving everywhere to surrender themselves to him with joyous hearts, opening their minds to his inspirations." (*Evangelization* par. 75)

Writing in 1979, Pope John Paul II described the role of the Spirit in these words: "Only the Spirit enables us to pray to God: 'Abba Father'. Without the Spirit we cannot say: 'Jesus is Lord'. From the Spirit come all the charisms that build up the Church, the community of Christians. In keeping with this, St. Paul gives each disciple of Christ the instruction. 'Be filled with the Spirit'." (*Cathechesis* par. 72)

The aim of this daily prayer is to help those who use it, to experience the
— indwelling
— guidance
— gifts
— and activity
of the Holy Spirit, in a renewing way.